taria è già un ... come corpo, in quanto nel
messaggio cri ... almente con la sal-
vezza per l'ir ... ale il singolo è inse-
rito. Appunto per la ... Dio pre...ede ogni azione e la
stessa fede da ... popolo di Dio, il singolo non resta mai solo. ... ...munità, la Chiesa, la
quale è essenzialmente di più della s... ...ei singoli...

Questo aspetto dell'alleanza, come legame f...iano-giuridi-
co che regola il rapporto tra il membro... il popolo di Dio, tra il
cristiano e la Chiesa, ha un risvolto anche per il p.no matrimoniale. Anche se non si parla più del rapporto singolo comunità
christifide lis et Ecclesia, ma dell'unità di due persone in rapporto al ... comun..., eccle...la, rimangono valid. due dati: ...
per la matrimoniale tra persone libere due che si uniscono in
matrimonio. Esse, nel costituire una persona, sono relazionate
ecclesia... In virtù di ... ...ono anch'esse far parte della
...mità ecclesiale, in virtù di ... Dio...mini, in mine..., des... ...
part...ghere, attraverso il segno che li unisce in questo v.ncolo.

... può essere a più di un solo coniugato, come se fosse
un coniuge più forte ri...ess.. dell'altra ...dizione dell'altro
... ...tata a D.o... ...la comunità osservata
gli a... nella comunità ecc...des...la... sia come membri p...de...
...no chiesu... nel esprimere la loro... ... ... d...
brev tra Jah.ve ed il suo popolo... ... ... tra Cristo... ...nta...
dele visibili al mondo.

Essi vengono chiamati ad inchinare ... amore fedele e perma-
nente, ape.to anche alla relazione con un terzo termine che si
concretizza in un'altra persona: il figlio.

Il figlio viene a parte.ipare dell'amore... ...ore del genitore. ...
Per mezzo suo, l'amore degli sposi è presen... da ciò che una
passione esclusiva esclusa in se stessa potrebbe ...ere: divide...
...iutica. L'altro coniuge non è più ...un...o... sarà necessario
'ognuno si apre di un terzo, il figlio.'

Robert North S.J.

GOLDEN AGE ODE

and other verses mostly on biblical archeology

ROME 2004

E R R A T A

p.61	**he** not she ⟋	line 6
51	west **and** [rhyme] **east**	5
4	**Afr.Am.My** not Ammy	22
9	*déjà vu*	end
53	Corfù	7
9**2**	w**h**ile not wile; **Sh**aria not Sah ᵃ	
117	**III** not **V** Royal Farmland	8
52	name take**n**	9
102	Yalvač	18
55	Not Arab **save for** few	5
125	books **and** in	14
112	Far **from** their	19

58.62.89.119 could,clods,feasts,peeved:
rhymes for end of preceding line .
114   box, rearranged as 4 col.2,25-28
59.11,30.72,74..75: ❝ [for A]; ⁓ [for B]

© 2004 – E.P.I.B. – ROMA

ISBN 88-7653-622-1

EDITRICE PONTIFICIO ISTITUTO BIBLICO
Piazza della Pilotta, 35 - 00187 Roma, Italia

PREFACE

Though having enjoyed exceptional college training in both Greek and English poetry, I was assigned to biblical archeology in Rome and conducting Mid-East study tours. Retirement convinced me that my best insurance against oncoming immobility was return to poetry study and publication, not for fame or money, but for public criticism.

I soon discovered that poetry journals, even if accepting rhymed though chiefly free verse, indicated their authors as almost exclusively college poetry professors or graduate students, who moreover had already published in two or three similar journals. Perhaps not all may favor my insistent condensing of each verse-line into a single printed line.

It had not dawned on me that my rejected contributions usually had a religious twist, mild not passionate like Hopkins, and ecumenical not creedal. Upon reconsidering the secularist trend and increasing "separation of church and state(-schools)", it seemed fairer to publish my verse as frankly religious, focussing biblical excavation areas and worldwide social justice.

My Provincial encouraged my project and agreed to an eventual subsidy for publication even after my normally-foreseeable death. For his generosity I am chiefly grateful; and also for the memory of my classmate Leonard Waters, who tutored me unstintingly before going on to initiate generations of Jesuits in English poetry.

Robert North S.J.

4

CONTENTS

GOLDEN AGE ODE
in ten self-standing Cantos

CANTO I: TIMES CHANGE, WE CHANGE

Ours is the season of life in which seniors gather together
              Nowadays most
Resting in caregivers' hospices, savoring comfort and weather
              Freedom their boast
Save for a few taken in by a family member left lonely
              Hospitable too;

Plus Third World households of blood-ties resolved to share only
              Poverty true.

      Each generation has its special ethos
          Shown in achievements, also in its games.
      "I care not who may make a nation's laws,
         So I may make its songs" old Pindar claims.
            The Roaring Twenties were our background style
          As teens and pre-teens; that was quite a while.

                     School-days, rule days,
                           We can recall;
                     Childish crush-days,
       The silent films, and songs of radio's first thrall.

When you and I were young, Maggie:
         Always, Blue Heaven, America God Bless!
Flappers charlestoned Till Three
         King Tut imaged the world's dress.
          My Prayer, O Johnny, Barrel Roll --
         Till Flowers Gone, in Yellow Ribbon stole.
           We felt the Crash,
               Then the Depression;
          Started out brash
              From school's last session,
        To make a life mid sorely testing pression.

For some a ray of light was F.D.R and W.P.A.
    Then came another war with losses more than gains;
But striving to acquire the atom bomb, they say,
      Brought us the computer and relief for many pains,
        By medics' funded progress in relieving soldiers' ills,
Which from Viet-Nam's failures in our life now helpful spills.

                    Adulthood brought peace
                    And prosperity
              Though we could not cease
                To plan and foresee
What status in our feeble days we might yet see.

                So now it has arrived
                And how lucky we are
              That fate for us contrived
                  Advantages so far
              Ahead of other nations
              And previous generations.

                Thank we our Lord
                  And relatives dear
              And a countless horde
              Of friends we revere
Who as far as is permitted remain to us so near.

Contacts of course are quite few in our actual situation,
But we can surely keep striving with cheeriest conversation
And some helpfulnesses suited to our feebler limitation
            To show our inner peace,
            And gratitude increase,
For so sublime a blessing as this our new Life's Lease

CANTO II: WE STRUCK GOLD

Ours is a humanly unprecedented development in history
For the aged and ill.
Life-lengthening pharmaceuticals, never before such to see,
Bring us a thrill;
Toil-percent pensions; insurances legislated socially
Plus Medicare still.
Hospices merciful, also "assisted living", though for a fee,
But kindness with no bill.

We struck it rich; just in our time
And in our vast but small percent
Of earth, prevails the prime
Of health and comfort, surely meant
To bring security not just for us
But for all sharers in our old-age fuss.

No ingrates we!
To Providence
Our thanks; and glee
For opulence
As our divinely-destined eminence.

This fortune blest is surely merited
Clearest of all by heirs of onetime slave;
But also by the ethnic groups, whose dread
Of structures in their homeland made them brave
To seek within our hospitable shore
Their Promised Land, a home for evermore.

Our thanks be shown
By joy at sharing
Not with "our own"
Only, but daring
To claim all as our own, with love and caring.

Is it not ours to query? why there should be chosen
Along with Europe's fraction of Earth's population
Our smallish quarter-billion, such as scarcely shows in
A map of all the billions in many a poorer nation.
It seems unfair, yet here too must be humbly heard
"My ways are not your ways" as God's revealing word.

At least we may
Acknowledge that
Our fortune's ray
And tender pat
Is just incentive to bring others where we sat.

Some few in any slot
Are luckier always
And richer too, but not
Happier in other ways;
God's gift not oft its counterpart portrays.

Luke's banker gave to one
For using while away
Thousands; almost none
To another; who could say
What his returning verdict will display?

Hard for a rich person Heaven to gain is our Gospel decree.
Yet we have faith that all who are rich with some generosity
"Poor in the Spirit" can hopefully face a reward in eternity.
                    We will use our luck
                    Tranquilly, yet with pluck
        Will do the best we can for all in misery stuck.

CANTO III: WHY FOR U-S SUCH LUXURY?

Why should the aged of one single nation be so far ahead
                            Of the rest of an earth
Starved not for food alone but for help against illnesses dread,
                            And in poverty's dearth
Never in hope of the medicines needed to hold up life's thread
                            In a dignified worth ?

                The answer seems plain: it's because
                    We inherit a land rich and vast,
                Conquered by struggles and laws
                    (Not to mention our slaves of the past);
                        But chiefly by skills and inventions
                        And progressive wealth/labor extensions.

                            Our Constitution
                                Claims equal all,
                            Not destitution
                            Nine-tenths world pall
                While our small wealthy crowd holds them in thrall.

                "Cannot all see how generous in grain
            And cash we are to backward lands?" we boast;
                Yet such "gifts" bring: to U.S. producers gain,
            Enslavement humbling to the world's most,

Kept from development and helpful trade
By laws our lobbyists and vote-seekers made.

Those poor lands see
Leftover scraps
All enviously
Despised as traps
By menace of"withholding" from their laps.

All hail to labor-unions, farmers, bankers' skills,
Whose capital brought TV for Third World dearth.
But hopes to find relief from hatred due to ills,
Require demanding, not just yielding, for all the earth
Access to export and import of goods adjusted
To their economies, not by "Made in USA" flat busted.

Preeminent, the sick
Of the two-thirds world
By economics' trick
To deeper anguish hurled,
Deserve aid medicines at prices downward twirled.

Lawmakers grant "Okay.
On one condition: that
Within the U.S.A.
Our living standard fat
Go down not one iota,
Hawaii to Dakota".

"Alas, blind guide
Your 'gifts' we spurn",
Sufferers replied,
"Until you learn
Equality for all men is with some cost to yearn."

Really at stake is the carrot and stick of world empire's power
Claiming to bring"help and peace" where U.S. "interests" flower,
"Striking preemptively",dictating any "regime change's" hour !
Sick seniors too: confess

Vote-bribe "costing you less"
Must aim toward fairer parity with foreign mess.

CANTO IV: RELIGIOUS TRADITIONS

Sacred to all is Religion, one's own: though a world with but one
Is our hope and our dream.
Eight-some are mainstream, but hundreds of others deep thinking
have done
On respect which they seem
All to accord to old age as a model and guide like the sun.
Let's skim off their cream.

Seventy is our normal span,
Psalm Ninety says in its Verse Ten
Maybe past eighty if we can,
Mostly the "weaker sex", but men
Can sometimes make it, with distress
And medicines, we must confess.

Akin is the norm
Even today
Despite reform
Of medics' way
With pills aplenty in hospices to stay.

Six other Psalms give little else that warns
About old age, save that it needs respect
And is a status lucky folk adorns.
Job's comforters add more about defect
And guilt of stubborn age; the Wisdom books
Claim prudent youths their own, not graying looks.

Such is the sum
Of Bible lore;
Five Prophets come
With brief hints more;
Taunts Joel: the oldsters dream, the young explore.

The Christian Gospel adds not much to these accepted views.
But Qor'an also is a biblically founded source.
By practice therefore must be judged each faith's Good News:
Islam perhaps accords a nobler vital force
To doddering age than westward-oriented Jews,
But in all three so-called "Bible monotheisms"
Aloof respect prevails, as in their many schisms.

Confucians and Africans do
          What helps the aged live;
Buddhists and Hindus too
          A fine example give;
If we can "yin-yang" or "no-name god" forgive.

The Amerindian's "untutor'd mind",
Says Alexander Pope, "sees God in cloud
          Or hears" his skyey Manitou "in wind".
Young braves faced instant death shouting aloud
          Obedience to their oldest toothless chiefs,
          And reverenced them as key to their beliefs.

                    Lip-service then at least
                              All faiths offer the old.
                    Many a group and priest
                              More actively unfold
                    Some charitable caring, church-controlled.

Conversely, touching religiousness what are the elders to say?
Now as they near their life's end, they should gather and pray.
Yet with Aloysius should add "Let us live while we may;
          A good life-style of which we are fond
          Is perhaps the most suitable wand
          For hope of forgiveness and welcome beyond".

CANTO V: WISDOM SHAM AND TRUE

Solomon's Wisdom 4,9 long ago quite expressly declares
                                    Unapocryphally!
Wisdom is not automatic along with the gray, white, or no hairs;
                                    And people agree:
Wiser a sensible kid than an elder who's putting on airs
                                    Somewhat totteringly.

          Old age for wisdom is acclaimed,
          Yet where's a scope for wise old gleams ?
          Is it a mere encomium named ?
          A euphemism for dreary dreams
          While toil and exploit all remains
          On younger shoulders, legs, and brains ?

                        What then to do
                            Wise to appear?
                        Have we a clue,
                            Facing all fear,
          True wisdom to display, with joy and cheer ?

          Tell folks to quit just flattering us as wise
          Meaning residual heritage of our past.
          Perhaps the time has come to recognize
          With Socrates the wisdom we've amassed
          Is to admit how ignorant we are
          And seek more truth out like a sinking star.

Ay, there's the rub
Sage is the one
Who joins the club
Of those whose fun
Is just to seek out truth that others shun.

Can't we be like Ulysses, who had sense to see
The "wise" is he who feels it's not too late for him
To seek out ever newer worlds relentlessly,
The knowledge which is sadly still beyond his rim ?
Not only technological and atom-splitting:
Arts and divine science too new heights are hitting.

Hail to the Wise
Truly, not fake;
Searching the prize
For which they ache;
Disclaiming poses others for us make.

So "Learn a bit each day"
The ancient proverbs plead.
Successfully we may
All obstacles impede,
And bravely set our mind
Improvement still to find.

While there's life there's hope
A new key to discern:
Not drearily just mope,
But youth's approval earn
By joining them in search for what to learn.

Ours is a life set for prayer, it is true, and for heavenly hope.
Still, it's a "Life before death", for a something that's worthy
our scope:
Some thought-work of notable value for which we can grope.
Let's use our mind:
Seek what's behind
The news, the universe, whatever we can find !

CANTO VI: THE LIFE-CYCLE

So-called "Extended family"used to be humankind's life-cycle
normal: It worked very well
Through the millennial village-and-farm-cultures, where the
informal Needed tasks fell
Just to whichever had strength and experience or training more
formal: For kids it was swell
Lambs to be chasing; adults could so varyingly storm all
Jobs, and problems dispel.

In each plain home and family
Were youth, age one to twenty;
Grandparents two or three,
And aunts or uncles plenty:
All helping out each other,
And dutiful to Mother.

Appreciated, wanted,
Living in harmony,
By squabbles small undaunted
Welcome and feeling free,
The oldest and the feeblest more especially.

How different condominiums in our skyscraping cities!
Folks off afar from dawn to dusk, most earning, some in
schooling,
Breadwinners male no longer: both sexes, and some
teenage pretties
No room for auntie now or grandpa in the emptied nest a-ruling.
Newlyweds quickly flee from the parental supervision,
And soon plan carefully dear ones' old-age provision.

Families no longer
Toil together. In essence
Love, they claim, is stronger
For a certain pleasance
In release from chafing too-protracted presence.

The clan-type family no more
Can hold out promise to the aging;
Indeed, they themselves implore,
War for their independence waging
Mid proliferating electronic
Conveniences, visual too and sonic.

Grandchildren dearest
Still lovingly come
To visit, and sheerest
The joy is when some
Tell of school or games or learning to drum.

We cannot change the tide
    Of history. If we could,
We still might glad abide
    The changes, and we would
      Impede them not; we come to feel
      They are for us a better deal.

                    Our culture's charms
                      "The American way",
                    Has its alarms,
                        Yet we can say
              It suits us, though it be not here to stay.

Are we to say just "farewell not goodbye" to the extended family,
Homes with a few generations together in mild harmony?
Who can say? Yet what is, can be best, says a critical philosophy.
                    For us, at any rate,
                    The die is cast, and fate
              Treats us too well, whatever we await.

CANTO VII: THE GENERATION-GAP

Proverbs says "Glory of youths is their strength, but of age frosty
                                        pow",
                    In twenty, two-nine.
But the last word of the whole Hebrew Bible, as we must allow,
            Is "Power divine [Mal 4,6]
Will turn the kids' views toward their dads'; dads' too somehow
            Toward the upcoming vine".

            With our now bygone century came
                Youth-oriented culture, and
            The spending-power children could claim
                From Internet-style ads so grand,
            To shield parents from kids' pouting
            In two-sex business world just sprouting.

                        How could one try
                            With scold and rod ?
                        Or lurk and spy
                            To stem the prod
                Of over-affluent trends and death of God ?

            From all the world to rich U. S. A. streamed
        Drugs honey-sweet death-dealing; overpowered
                All hope of pristine discipline, nor gleamed
        Some spark of parent guide for youth thus showered
                By furtive fun and games, with sex thrown in.
                Elders "just don't understand" and prate of sin.

Not all is glum:
Children abound
With dad and mum
Strolling around
And learning to behave from counsels sound.

What place have ancients in a modern world of youth ?
Well, parents long ago caught on, even complained:
Grandparents spoil the children and win them, that's the truth.
This can relieve some dads and moms so stressed and pained
By overdone careers, no time for home at all:
Grandma can baby-sit, gramps teach to throw a ball.

That's the ideal,
But Medicare
Hospices the real
Life oldsters share,
Putting them far from home with children there.

Children are trained to muse
"Steer clear of grownup strangers:
They kidnap or abuse".
But parents see no dangers
When bent gray shufflers win
A sympathetic grin.

The generations three,
Not two, help to disarm
The gap, and thus set free
Parents from some alarm
And add some insight into childish charm.

Ours is the same old young-people's world that it was from the
start,
Charms of the children win over and lull their guardians' heart,
Some of the old and some of the young still foster the art
Of mutual understanding
And patient oustretched-handing
Each other to togetherness expanding.

CANTO VIII: WAITING ? OR UP AND DOING?

We are here in this condition for a purpose, with a mission,
And we have a slight suspicion it is something worth our
steel.
Is it just "awaiting death"? or--a performing we still have breath
for?
There's a veritable plethora of tasks we can't conceal:
Cheering some worse off than we?
Scribbling reams of poetry?
Praying for society?
Where our taste or talent lies !

Not a goal but a marker of our steps toward some real sparker
Is the grave with something darker it undoubtedly contains.
Should we gather up our forces while we cast aside remorses,
Not just sit and hold our horses: doggedly face what remains?
       Clapping for the Cards or Packers?
       Pushing at the statesmen-slackers?
       Writing to the wrong-side backers?
       Things to do beneath the skies.

           In past years perhaps
              We held spellbound
          Audiences or chaps
             In school or playground
                 Or were mechanics skilled,
                 Or milliners that thrilled.

     Arthritis grips our fingers,
   Or lively memories fade us;
     Deafness hits great singers,
 Concentrations jade us
But active still are some few skills quite real
Not only market-values now to us appeal.

But loftier aims at what may yet improve our mind:
Newspapers offer more than comics or just how
Some bum was murdered. In them we can find
Nuggets of usefulness for here and now
Crosswords and other puzzles to enjoy,
Or recipes to win the hungry boy.

To classics we may turn,
Of music or of art;
Famed novelists may earn,
A place within our heart:
To each his own, a culture-space apart.

And there's a whole wide world to aid,
At least applauding the enlisted
In care-societies which upgrade
The desperate nations, and two-fisted
Fighters against wrong legislation
Aimed to keep us wealthiest nation.

One more active task
The most momentous is:
In hours of prayer to ask
God's concern for his
Messed-up creation: after all, God's biz.

Bravely then must we decide if we only should patiently wait
Stroke of Grim Reaper, or rather prepare some, suiting our state,
Offering as last contribution to help out our world and its fate.
It gives life a meaning,
While soul we are cleaning,
And God's own ways are carefully screening.

CANTO IX: RESISTING? OR ADAPTING ?

Heaven, by Jewish and Christian awaited, was early conceived as
During an age when the sky was all up, and all hell below was
                                        believed as.
Now any notion that Earth is immobile and centrical Science
                                        relieved has.
                        Nor is our universe
                        Man-centered: the reverse
            Earth's an off-center pinpoint even worse.

                    All these discoveries scientific
                    Forced faith to some rethinking,
                    Not always beatific;
                    Nay, to resistance sinking:
                        Columbus, Galileo, Evolution
                        Each seen as hostile revolution.

                        Time heals all ills.
                        The Holy See
                        Tore off the frills,
                        Faced reality:
                Apologized for its ill-based hostility.

So now what is that heaven we soon await as true ?
        Not up in sunny daytime, down at night, for sure.
And what about the risen bodies: old, young, or new ?
        Greek soul's immortality was not the Christian lure.
Nor harps and cherubs, chats with Mom, and blessed gaze:
Anthropomorphic imaginations on which our mind could graze.

        Doubtless "something like that"
            But the known facts are few,
        Our faith is mystery flat,
            Which all tradition knew
            As unexplainable to human view.

Heaven's joy lies in possessing God;
        In that we fully can confide;
But put in terms for minds that plod
        Is something else; at best we hide
Ultimate reality in imaginings
And loving hopes all drawn from earthly things.

            This is not wrong
                Or bad; emotion
            And heart must long
                For our fond notion
Of heavenly reward as crown of our devotion.

Not Science alone makes progress; the most orthodox theology
            Must "change in order to remain the same";
            Gets duly, soberly reformulated:
In terms to changing language-use adapted is our plea:
            Deeper than just "what's in a name ?":
            Archaic phraseology re-stated,
            And even in legitimate ways updated.

Not Heaven alone; Hell too
Must be re-thought.
Hell amply is the loss of God !
All fire, pain, howling, demons' crew
Are from imagination brought;
To think God being "satisfied" is odd.
Or "Hell is beautiful,
For it fulfils God's plan".
Though to Faith's laws dutiful:
Let's not ascribe to God the vengefulness of man.

And Purgatory fire fate
"Invented" rather late,
With it brought Indulgences and spared
Survivors anguish: let their coins abate
The time-bound pains of their dear ones, who dared
Live recklessly: -- can they be aided
By money ? It's a human comfort,
Still legal, after the protests paraded
By Luther's not entirely unbased retort.

Heaven is God; this we know and it elegantly suffices;
Scarce matters what we may dream of how a "reward" equalizes
Injustice and pangs of earth's life which to heaven entice us.
Lazarus felt no better
Knowing Dives in fetter.
How could vengeful glee change divine joys by a letter?

CANTO X: HEAVEN'S CHASING HOUND

"God that just won't go away" may be Newberg's quite recent
                                        expression
For what Francis Thompson delineates as human depression,
Struggling for pitiful joys in despite of unceasing possession
                        Of an unremitting Voice
                        That leaves to us no choice
Between realizing our destiny and straying to rejoice.

            Our dark days, after all,
                    And loss of all we treasure
            Are shade of his footfall,
                    Who alone can measure
How he saved up for us what seemed our only pleasure.

        Whether we named him Elohim/Allah (same word)
Or borrowed Greek "theism" sans poly-;
            Or in our various Norse languages preferred
Goth, Gut, or God with normally linguistic folly:
                    No matter, child, the name:
                    Our origin/goal are the same
As what others call Manitou, Yin-Yang, the Nameless, or the
                                        Atheism ploy
Which Greeks hung on us Christians for denying their many theoí

But that Divinity chasing us
And shrouding us with dark,
Has still another title facing us
Among those mid which we grope.
We call him "the Father of Jesus"
Claiming that all should hark
To that Name in which humankind must hope.
And this has led to confrontations
With the faiths of other nations,
Until Ecumenism in our day
Shone forth with papal blessing,
Aiming to show how God revealed some ray
Of his true self to other names confessing.

Our God is Mystery,
Our faith too not just history;
Which we ourselves demand
No human mind can really understand
But we with equal firmness claim
Religions should unite,
In peace, not hatred. Shared limits we can aim
And this has realigned our missionary policy:
Sympathy and openness, not fight,
Can best lead others toward the Light!
Within our faith as well we ought to recognize
Its mysteriousness, and be wary of imposing
As the content of faith's prize.
Our imaginative approximations
Or formula-bound disclosing

All these humanly desired declarations
We'll fulfil though otherwise
In the Happy Hunting Ground
Where faith gives place to sight.
This is not syncretism
Or rank indifferentism;
No; frank acknowledgment of today's Dark Night.

The first great Law thus turns out
Quite like the Second:
"If we cannot show concretely

Love for neighbor whom we see,
How can we love the God whom we cannot ?"
And won't this realization be
Veritably fecund
In guaranteeing our eternal destiny ?
Loving fellowman First Prize was Adhem's
lot.

Our end is coming fairly soon,
Our recognized eternal goal.
Just when, just how we'll get this boon
And save our own rewarded soul --
All that is God's not quite decipherable scroll.
"Up there" we shall hear oft repeated
"What you did for the needy was done
All for Me", --Our entreated
"Mercy! Forgiveness!" gets this reply, only one.
But in this we'll find all
That we lived for: the call
To fulfilment sufficient forever to enthral.

New Canticle for Oldsters' New Year

The Spirit cries "I make everything new",
And that means people also, me and you.
What day could this renewal better be
Than nature's own each-yearly jubilee?

How could our liturgy blot out entire
What folk-traditions avidly desire?
A day so rich in moral sentiment,
With kids' resolves "Make this year different".

We know the answer, and we fight to save
Vanishing Advent from its yawning grave.
Yet Church New Year so otherwise conceived
Leaves space for one folks natcherly believed.

Our secular yet heaven-centered year
Starts with a dream of all new faces near.
With memories of "new kid upon" our block
Who raised our hope of friendly culture-shock.

So we would dream that New Year signifies
New faces round us easier to prize.
Not just life-cycle norms to bring us here
The faces that replace gone ones so dear.

But each of us with God's renewing grace
May eagerly "paint on a happy face".
How nice to come into the dining-room
And see on every phiz no trace of gloom.

Face-painting thus comes only from the heart,
Not all so slyly wield the brush of art.
Far easier to think how others to improve
Than how my own too stolid features move.

Youth's ornament of course is chatty joy
We're past the age such weapons to employ.
Technology may yet the giftie gie us
To see ourselves as hidden cameras see us,

That when we gather for some so-called fun
A brightened face may show on every one.
All frowns and wrinkles glowering in December
By January's wand made cheeriness to remember.

Good Friday and September Eleventh still have place
But need not drive the sunshine from our face.
We'll still have faults yet think a better world
Is one with varying characters unfurled.

      We don't see many darling children, yet
      With maturer charms around we need not fret.
      So may our New Year's resolution be
      That comrades who have only us to see

Instead of cherubs, glimpse upon our face
A pleasant reassuring light of grace.
And what we thought was others' frowning glare
Is just the love they're trying hard to share.

      May New Year's Day bring joys of its good fairy,
      Along with undiminished praise of Mary.
      And may this octave of her Bethlehem child
      Keep us all year more generous and mild.

Maverick Insights on Third-World Aid

Formalist's Ross Coggins on Development,
Hilariously cynical, is yet intent
To focus one or other paradox
With valid lessons even while it knocks.

> Unmasked, his shocking true contention is
> That World Aid Projects foster U.S. Biz,
> Bringing the "donors" costly comforts while
> The "beneficiaries" get scarce a smile.

Each "gift" a product paid in U.S.A.,
Local nature-resource gives foreign pay.
And even peace corps or religious groups
Unwarily get caught in profit-loops.

> Examples : noblest aims to help the masses
> Are chatted out amid the higher classes.
> Drawbacks to each solution bring good eating,
> By fostering yet a posh restaurant meeting.

In Hiltons: multinationals are cursed;
"Hotbeds of social rest" yield protests worst.
To focus malnutrition, order steaks ;
With esoteric terms, give poor the breaks.

Development Set home photographs assure
Leaders no less at ease with great than poor
God's promise backs a lasting well-paid mission:
"There's always some in destitute condition".

From every dime to mitigate despair
Just what percent increases incomes fair ?
So what's new if the starving envious
Doubt "Our aim: make you as well-off as us".

Farm-Pharm

Two needful mainstays of our daily life
Are food and medicine, yet they bring strife
Of different kind, with those who aid would pitch
To starving folk enviously blaming us rich.

Farms are no longer toilsome family plots
But supervised vast acreages, with lots
Of costly high-tech machinery.
Yet drouth or flood still menace all their greenery.

So Congressmen mindful of votes from states
Like Iowa contrive the subsidy which rates
Low-priced sales abroad and kills the competition
Of surplus rare in neighbor third-world position.

Pharmakon means poison, now used to heal:
Not herbs and poultices medieval, but real
Miracle drugs perfected by researching teams,
Expensively-trained thousands actuating dreams.

Their top-range wages are a small percent
Of the multinational companies', naturally bent
On profit, though their finds bring huge relief
To sufferers rich enough to soothe their grief.

Philanthropists and nations really try
To help the sufferers who find the price too high;
Yet their generous dollars and euros go
Chiefly to swell multinationals' cash-flow.

Globalization is truly in a bind:
Escape from two dilemmas somehow find:
Fix change-rates to sad local economies
Yet not defraud meritorious companies.

Or personalizing more humanely, how
To get the food and drugs to needers now
Yet with fairness to expensively schooled toil
Of pharmaceutists, bankers, and farmers' soil.

Vers Libre and Hopkins

Free Verse origins, says Steele, were wholly French
Where rigidly (unglimpsed in Anglo trench)
Alternate rhymes must end "female", unvoiced -e.
No such straitjacket in English verse had we

Hence the claimed "whole first twenty years free verse
All French", was hid agenda: freed from something worse
Than nix to an occasional extra syllable
Or short with long in English always fillable.

"Sprung rhythm" claimed by Hopkins as his own
Admits enumerated precedents in tone,
And yet is ranged with free verse avant-garde:
A "freedom" long enjoyed by British bard.

Yet more at stake is the "poetic fire",
Dazzling word-choice to which poets aspire,
Here Hopkins boldly leads with metered rhymes,
Chiefly by patterned sonnets, many times.

"Prose" for "free verse" is shunned as dirty word
Yet its "free rhythm" vaunted "naturally" heard.
Truth is, Greek poetry came first, and prose
Long after strove to imitate just how it goes.

Not by Hopkins only avoided in discussion
But unconcealed are the non-percussion
Factors like print-invented visuality,
"USA best!", and Science "new is better" plea.

"Revolt against meter" quietly fought by Steele
Genuine merits of free verse does not conceal
Yet e'er between the lines the question rose
"Is it after all so different from prose?"

Pharaoh

Our Bible leaves unnamed some Egypt kings
(Egyptian title "Big House" like our "White House" rings)
Once about Jacob's Joseph and the dreams
Of seven-year famine eluding schemes.

Four centuries (or generations?) later came
The Moses-Pharaoh: Tutmoses Third some claim;
Too soon or late, our scholarship avers
And glorious Ramses Second prefers

As killer of all Jewish baby boys:
But his own daughter saved Moses mid her toys
Then brought him up in Pharaoh's family
Till as adult he fought kin-Jews to free.

Not Ramses but his son Menephta then
Was Pharaoh, experts say, before whose men
Moses as outlaw fled to Sinai-waste
There Yahweh's true name and mandate to taste.

With Menephta, using snakes and plagues, his plea
He parleyed, winning: "Set my people free !'
Reed Sea crossed and on the Sinai peak
Received the Ten Commands to help the weak.

Such is the gripping tale before us now,
Whether as history, in part ?or how ?
Or as religious parable, the wise debate:
Yet through the ages faithfully narrate.

Nile Railway

Early explorers found it to their taste
On stately houseboats time and funds to waste.
All pyramids and frescoed tombs, it's true,
Are near the Nile and handily to view.

But now the railway gives an imposing show
Of landscapes, and quick easy ways to go
From Alexandria almost to Abu Simbel
With stops unnumbered for inquirers nimble.

At dusk from Cairo on the moving train
Enjoying supper, noting without strain
A dozen pyramids, then time for bed,
For dawn at Luxor, or go on instead.

Snoozing past Minya, Beni Hassan frescoes and
Junction for Fayum, only non-Nile oasis-land.
Population centers of recent history
Along the rail have no antiques to see.

But from express-stop at Mallawi, or nearer,
With effort and Nile-crossing, to the dearer
Amarna painted floors and donkey-ride
To Akhetaten frescoes of the sun-rays' pride.

Nag-Hammadi: but too far in railway planning
Is Chenoboskion, site of recent scanning
Of Thomas-"Gospel" and cognate momentous
Syriac manuscripts now in Cairo to content us.

Still north of Luxor, Balyana-stop would merit
A visit of Abydos remains, and one should share it
With time and toil for Idfu temple south, as also
For famed "Double Façade" of Kom Ombo.

For most, Nile Railway and Egypt itself is just
Luxor: Karnak temples; lone Ozymandias bust,
Hatshepsut's Temple, Valley of the Kings
Whose art and power unforgotten clings.

Finally Aswan, Elephantine in script-finds rich,
Gives access to "dammed" Philae island, and the niche
Of the Unfinished Obelisk's old quarry,
And cruel techniques of pharaonic glory.

Deerslayer

Unundestandable how Fenimore Cooper
Can be so readable and ingratiating;
True, into Indian lore he's a deft snooper:

But his hero rambles on in endless prating
Preachily to tough guys far from sharing
His wise ideals: ethnic collaborating

And God-sent "gifts", in Indians rather scaring.
But somehow those long page-or-more discourses
Are so sincere and fit his heroic bearing,

His so-successful activities with horses,
Fur-trapping, and escape from bad guys' plots
That we can't but admire his moral forces

And wish our selfish world would have lots
Of altruistic idealists such as he.
No murderous gunplay his character blots:

For this called "(Only) deer"-slayer, and we
Favor the "Pathfinder" as he's sometimes named,
Though "Leatherstocking" he's supposed to be.

Amazing that a novelist so rightly blamed
For bland archaic style, and so centuries old
Today so ardently could still be famed,

And with more recent gestes of cowboys bold
In Grade-A Westerns of our day compared,
Though Hollywood has not yet taken hold

Like Ivanhoe, he earns attentive gaze
For waking those in cruel backgrounds snared
To inborn human nobility deserving praise.

Rumbling Around Inside

"Unconscious cerebration" is a lucky grind
Of our creatively disposed mentality;
Small seed bouncing around inside our mind

While sleeping or distracted during lectures, we
Can flesh it out toward what we hoped to find.
As "Insight" or "Inspiration" oft identified.

How much we owe to unreasoning synapses
In that gray matter cranium can hide:
Even at times in discourteous lapses

Of attention at dull meetings. or when pride
Of central focus at awards collapses
Into "Eureka" of some missing link
Which effort can't enable us to think.

Not poets only. Engineers are blocked
In planning giant bridges or skyscrapers
By some detail, until some dawn they're shocked

To see solutions. For inventive capers
Of an Edison in unsurmounteds locked
Not 99% sweat but some lone papers

Bounce forth that resistant formula in sleep!
Detectives mid N false approaches too,
Or military strategists cautiously creep

Up, but find all unexpectedly the clue.
Our mental process unimaginably deep
Unreasoning oft hints what we should do.

So thank we all our Maker's sly provisions
Of this subhuman source of genius true,
Our cerebration's purely chance collisions.

Maverick Re-Thinking

Coggins I praised for rightly making fun
Of turgid upperclass executives, who gain
A comfortable salary with "perquisites", not one

But many, airborne globewide, to bring grain
And medicine to millions who daily run
The risk of death in infancy or pain.

For such they foster what he calls "development".
Chiefly by wrangling in the local inns
Most comfortable and costly; men intent

On aiding the poor masses, with some tins
Of foreign-tasting products and well-meant
Projects to exploit natural-resource bins.

No question of hypocrisy or pretense.
Yet we must wonder whence the money comes
Or goes: in rich men's pockets, what per cents ?

Undoubtedly quite interesting sums.
From governments, philanthropists, the rich.
To pay for Western goods: does that make sense?

Then to : "developers" and for "gifts" by which
They get much-needed "license" locally
From powerholders; to (healing) drug-diffusers
At prices sky-high for the desperate users.

This "rich to rich to rich" cycle must be
Broken -- without neglecting the just claims:
One: pharmaceutists; two: the farmers; three,

The congresses and parliaments, whose aims
Are : "Yes, we must reduce the envious hate
Of the third world; not by TV-games:

Help sincere, but always through the gate
Of winning votes by promising our own nation
Their wealth and comforts never to abate;

Develop local ores with consideration
Of local needs, but to us a good cash-flow".
Reform not brusquely but with moderation.

How could the modest farm or druggist show
For a plan that leaves them poorer, approbation ?
Though needed for far-off self-help to grow.

Can miracle-drugs ignore researchers' pay ?
Sore problems; yet the worst is change-rate fix
So Africans the Aids and cancer treatments may

Buy through the normal economic tricks.
Day's eighty-dollar wage U.S. or Sweden, say,
Is five, or one, for Hindu or Islamic hicks.

That makes our ten-dollar pill in their real worth
Sixty or twelve cents; imports should be priced
At that rate; but this would leave a dearth.

All hail to farmers; just a century ago
They kept us fed by struggle with the earth
Twelve hours a day with wife and children, though

Incessantly threatened by drouth or flood.
But things are different now as smoothly flow
The toils; no white or red scalpers seek blood;

Machinery vast acreages harvests quick;
Insurance compensates disasters' mud.
Do they now need tax-subsidies so slick?

Or payment for the crops they leave untilled?
To keep a global market for their grains
Though this means third-world competition killed.

Why should not "foreign aid" leave room for gains
From nearby nations' surpluses to build?
Thus really lessen starving third world pains.

Questionable perquisites for CEOs are small
Compared with these urgent farm-parities
And miracle-drugs at rated price to all

In need of Western so-called charities.
Thus ease the widespread envy-hatred thrall
On which thrive terrorists' barbaric glees

In Shah-Iran

A year before the Islamic revolution
Destituted the self-styled Shah, left him exiled
And hastened the Persian Gulf wars "solution",

   Our adult-student group cautiously filed
   Throughout Iran to glimpse its biblical
   Remains, in archeological interests mild,

   Leaving aside what Caspian sites enthral
   Historian-tourists of more recent date.
   First in assigned hotel we briefly lodged

In Tehran, whose museum could quite sate
Initial surveys. Then southward we dodged
Through glories of the nascent Islam-state,

   Isfahan and poetry-capital Shiraz;
   Mostly at near Persepolis involved,
   After Pasargadae and Cyrus' tomb.

   Darius at Persepolis evolved
   An "Apadana"-Palace, ample room
   For Xerxes' ethnic frieze, which solved

Neighboring peoples' garments, traits, and doom.
Four hundred miles northwest mostly survive
Artaxerxes' Susa and Bible-concerns:

   Find-site of Hammurabi, whence derive
   Exodus Covenant-laws; where Esther turns
   For Purim mercies; and are still alive

Memories of Daniel, even burial-urns.
Ecbatana, three hundred miles straight north,
Tobit's last home, is now called Hamadan,
Whence Cyrus' famed Jews-freeing scroll went forth.

Finally, westward, Bisitun cliff, on
Which only daredevil courage could unroll
From Greek beside, the tongues of Babylon.

Let us not overlook Zoroastrian Mazda's role
In imaging Judeo-Christian angels and heaven
Though dualism was spurned by Christian soul.
Nor Muslim-tolerated poetry of Iran
Which world-Islam admired and built upon.

Iliad 23 and Louis L'Amour

Achilles for Patroclus holds great funeral games
With prizes for each tough athletic sport:
Chariot-racing, boxing, wrestling, footraces he names.

Homer each hero-encounter, though in short
So punch-by-punch describes, it makes one think
About L'Amour's recent successful sort

Of Westerns.Slim young Good Guys at the brink
Of cruel catastrophe, most as in Zane Grey
Or Max Brand, sought by votaries of drink

And gambling, Bad Guys' vicious secret way
Of schemes to steal the lone maiden's ranch.
But hero's sly last-ditch ploy wins the day.

L'Amour to these themes adds his special branch;
From his prize-fight experience he can show
How a skilled boxer sees and grabs each chance;

In whole stories or lively digression go
Through such a match as a TV commentator.
Like Homer stressing bulk of boasting pro,

While challenger with shrewd strength bursts out later.
Homer, it's true, gives more ample spaces
With self-glorifying advice of oldish prater

On less punch/tackle-dependent races
But they too show a death-defying spice
Of tough and manly courage in their chases.

To turn from dime novel of pioneering West
To classic author's poetry beyond price
Describing Grecian athletes' pride and zest
Though slightly d,j... vu seems well expressed.

The Fertile Crescent

Archeology has brought to light
Centers of our concern in the Near East:
Roughly all form a crescent bright

Symbol, it happens, of the Islamic world,
But found in search of Abram's Bible-flight
North from Ur/Harran, through Twin-Rivers curled,

Our Mesopotamia, also coincidentally
By oil-deposit strife unceasing swirled;
And then through Syria south relentlessly

Well into Egypt, back to Canaan to settle.
Yet his line Jacob-Joseph soon we see
Again in Egypt, testing sore their mettle.

But many exegetes, disturbed to see no sign
Of "origins re-found" acknowledged in fine fettle
By exiles under Ezra, doubt Ur-source of the line

As later fiction; rather, some would say
Unrelated tribes in Canaan intertwine,
Applying to the "Union", in a way,

Separate traditions of some various tribes:
Far off from Ur one, maybe from Harran,
One to a friendly Egypt-stay ascribes,

Another held an Exodus to Midian,
Hebrews by hate and slavery circumscribes.
Moses, like name, is claimed Egyptian;

By others, Jews to Midian interwedding; Sinai is
   Jethro's turf; he's Yahweh's priest!
Howe'er it be, traditions all imbedding

These sites fit in a crescent with points south
   And body north, but bulging east and west
With Palestine a kind of brainy mouth

The desert in between can now be crossed
   By bus in one sole night despite the drouth
From Baghdad to Damascus safely tossed

Or farther north, via Dura-Europos synagogue,
   Palmyra Roman ruins farther west
Famed for Zenobia and camel-refreshing cog
   `To give our study of the Near East zest.

Greece and its Isles

Most folks reach Athens now by air or sea:
And marvel at its origins of our culture
Piraeus still just where it used to be;

A metal plaque of Paul's Pnyx lecture
Quite near Acropolis they now can see
"Unknown God"; below, Herod Atticus stage.

Westward, Eleusis famed for "Mysteries",
Name take over for many a Christian page.
And crossing bridged deep Isthmus gulf, one sees.

New Corinth, not near that of classic age.
Southward Mycenae, Sparta, Argos, Tiryns please;
Along the Gulf wends Patras railway to

Olympia of Games which now our fancy seize.
North cross the gulf, Lepanto roadway through
Most famed cult-center, on to Pindar's Thebes.

For Paul afoot the Macedon he knew,
With Philippi as entry-point was "Greece":
Thence west on Romeward Via Egnatia

Toward (Thes-)Salonike and Beroea he strolled,
Past Amphipolis and Apollonia.
Of islands, East-Aegean alone he told:

Samothrace, Lesbos now rather Mytilenia.
Ships leave Piraeus nightly; some are bold
And go far west to Delos, wholly shrine

Of nearby isles' "Amphictyony"; other boats
Serve isles like Paros with its marble fine.
But to apocalyptic Patmos near Ephesus floats

No cruise direct; only local sailboat line.
From Athens overnight to Crete steamboats
Wake you near Knossos and Minotaur's maze.

Far westward is Corcyra, now Corf—,

But if you would on Ulysses' homeland gaze,
Stop off at Ithaca, and pay your due

To wisdom's hero, and the centuries' praise.
Romantic and historic are these scenes, and others
Influencing the faith-forms of our Jew-sprung brothers.

The World of Islam

My Mid-East job in "Fertile Crescent" lay,
The Arabic-speaking Muslim nucleus. Though
Mecca was farther south, "power-centers" (we say)

Moved quick, Umayyad to Damascus. To Baghdad slow,
Abbasid leadership, with Iran-linked Shiite branch.
Then to the Fatimid claimants in Cairo.

Not Arabic but fervent, Ottoman Turkey got its chance
While also-near Iran had to content
Itself with lead in poetry and romance.

Libya to Morocco, North-African extent,
All Arab but with Berbers led the way
to massive Muslim Spain, soon mostly sent

Southward where Andalucia had its day:
Seville, Guadalquivir, and Cordoba
Boomed with architecture marveled still today.

Scholarship too, from Spain to India
Throve; our number-system with invented zero;
Avicenna, Maimonides, Aquinas–equal cathedra.

Al-Ghazzali a theologian's hero.
Chemistry as science really then begun;
History, geography the best since Nero!

Today more world-wide is Islam's full billion;
More faithful than secularized Christian West:
Doubtful if suicidal violence is its sillion.

Densest concentration in Indonesia guessed,
Not Arab few words in their planes.
Strong too in Filipino's southern isles.

Pakistan, Bangladesh; in India large remains
Far into Africa (from Mecca few gulf miles)
To Western world many an immigrant entrains
Some converts, Cassius Clay Mohammed ups smiles

The Arab Children

Much of my life in Palestine was spent
And desert lands adjacent, not with kings
Or scholars, but with laborious little things
Working on excavations; or from nearby tent

Boys for a school in circle on sands were sent
Like a fresh flower-garden, in shout or song;
Or on the train, a cheery youthful throng
Curious over the strange Mrikani bent.

In Israel I was helped by high-class groups,
And much admired their West-inspired bold
Firm government; their social equalizing,
Powerful allies and well-disciplined troops,
But excavation-help were mostly old
And I scarce knew the generation rising.

From Arab Gaza, Bethlehem, Jenin,
Now daily come preoccupying reports
Of boys manipulated in their sports,
To throw stones at Israeli guards just seen:
Challenging "self-protective" tanks to intervene.
No Arab leading power is strong enough
To discipline revolting gangs of tough
Child-inciters and prevent bloodshed obscene.

Those Arab kids! Who can hold back a tear
To think of their cruel background and sad fate?
Granted gangs claim to find no other way
The justice of their "homeland" claim to state.
A nation, not just kids, manipulated
By superpowers to gain ascendance fated.

Anticipation of U.S.A. Autumn 2002
in Homer's Iliad 2,1-40

The High God in a ticklish situation
Resolved to send his angel, Tricky Dream,
Disguised as best known Counsellor to seem,
To Ruler of the then most powerful nation,
Assuring success in instant armed invasion
No matter what all others should decide
Or secrets from his people he should hide. --
The High God knew this would bring tribulation

Or failure even, world-wide hostility;
This clear foreseeing, yet he thought it best
To leave decision to instruments involved,
For it was just Trick Dream, false though it be;
No fault of God if democracy's behest
Fell prey to moral imperatives unsolved.

Is Any African-American MyNeighbor?
(Love your neighbor as yourself: Lev 19,18; Who is my neighbor? Lk 10,29)

Toward interracial justice much is won.
But are we really neighbors? Care we whether
Apartheid neighborhoods exist; "birds of a feather",
Though thus they cannot grievous crime-rate shun
With "public" schools most black and seeking fun,
Not education, but congenial gangs
More formative than books or homes. What pangs
For teachers wrongly by low test-grades undone!

The youths too must be "understood" for claiming
"All we can get is too little compensation
For centuries of slavery, deprivation,
Insult"; nor will they accept our aiming
As "just to help them" toward assimilation
For many a goal more than for Kluxers shaming.

Whites also, though desiring honestly
Racial improvement, for their children's good
Choose private schools within their neighborhood
Or to the more congenial suburbs flee.
Solution can't be found realistically;
Bussing to other areas was tried, and
could Bring only crisis to high-quality childhood.
Church, media, politicos agree:

Why raise dilemmas which we cannot solve?
So ostrich-heads are buried in the sand
Of mute acceptance. God, how can our land,
Seek all its folk as neighbors to involve,
Not populate our prisons with one band,
The other still with luxuries absolve ?

Feminist Prodigal ?

A pushy biblical-updating fan
      Pro-feminist (not to re-make English new:
      German girls are neuter, Turk males too !)
Agreed the hero was too often man.
Even the world's greatest story ran
      In Luke "A certain Man had just two Sons".
      Why not one girl? or even both those ones ?
Or smuggle in a mother? or a nan?
      He variously tried: A roaming miss?
Too sexy. Widow divvying the family cash?
      A jealous unforgiving older sis?
      Belittling. None had just the proper flash.
Feminists, asked, burst into tears of rage:
A Cynic ridicule! Don't touch that perfect page".

The Prodigal Ten Years Later

Dan Lord, insightful Midwest youth-faith guide
      Skipped talk about the bad boy and mean bro;
      Instead asked how small-town life would go
After his chance in Babylon to bide.
Could he his wants and broader notions hide ?
      Farm-chores and meal-chat so boringly slow?
      Big Brother smug-reproachful, he might know.
Rare even to tame village-dance a ride.

After repentance and homecoming jigs,
      Things settled down to duty, duty, duty.
      No fun or winks at any local beauty.
No more his lazy freedom tending pigs,
      Penance enough was just his daily grind.
Prodigals, guard ! in making up your mind.

Hopkins and Wordsworth

Hopkins' "dearest freshness deep down things"
    Has the Wordsworth-praised terms of daily use
    Combined in twirls verging on abuse.
Elsewhere archaic or invented pings
His choice; arresting twist she brings:
    Oddments prized most as treasures of his Muse.
    Everyday speech too in his verse diffuse
He somehow with his vaunted "inscape" strings.
Wordsworth in tame order of daily prose
    Cannily his bewitching rhythms sets;
In complex rhyme-schemes long to short line goes,
    Into plain words some lyric outburst gets.
    Both kinds we need and ardently admire
    And toward Muse-given "dappled things" aspire.

Pharaoh Heretic

Egypt's King was tyrant, god, and priest,
Till Akhenaten just refused to go
Along with all that rigmarole, and so
From the tight priest-control he got released
By moving his bureaucracy at least
From Luxor to Amarna, though
Naming it Akhetaten, the Sun's glow;
His honor alone they'd henceforth feast.
Instead of jackals, cats, and other gods.
Frescoes and reliefs of the lifegiving Sun.
But such 'monotheism' sore irked the priestly
clods: They forced successor-boy
Tutankhamun
To excommunicate his heretic dad,
Regain Luxor and reimpose idols they'd had.

Roaming Edom and Moab

South of the Jordan, Arabalies dry
Till Eilat Red Sea inlet; eastward here
Came the Exodus crowd in route unclear

Past Brazen Serpent Pounon site. Hard by,
Rose-red Petra ruins monumental lie,
Nabatean caravan-center in Idumea drear,
Origin of Herod cruel without peer.
Northward Arnon Grand Canyon banks defy.

Here Moab's fluid boundaries begin:
Dibon of Mesha stela's many a line;
Nebo of Moses' punishment for sin
Near Madaba mosaic Palestine.
West Ammon; north Jerash, Jabbok stream
Pella, Gadara, and Galilee lake gleam.

Prose to Rhyme via Free Verse

Reaching three thousand lines in metre and rhyme,
Wondering open-minded why free verse takes
over :It was a bit embarrassing to discover
Suddenly and all-unbeknownst that I'm
A secret fan; for I've been all this time
Putting my thought for some lines in the clover
Of easy "lofty" prose, then as a rover
Supplying lacking rhymes.Is that a crime ?

Or has it been a valuable hint:
Free verse is not so different after all ?
Prose lined up with just a nobler tint
Is half the job of into rhyme to fall;
Can serve as useful bridge, and even perhaps
Reconcile adversaries by mediating flaps.

Obelisks

Twenty pharaonic obelisks survive
Only four in Egypt; London, Paris one,
Also New York and Turkey; but Rome alone
A dozen, to keep Earth-Rule's fame alive
Dragged off, yet left on rubbish-heaps to thrive
Till Renaissance Popes set them nobly grown
Upright, in Vatican, Lateran, Folk-square throne.
Their Bible-prized inscriptions bravely strive

To tell of Ramses, who killed the male-babe Hebrews
Save Moses, then adopted by his daughter;
Their elders to build store-cities would shackle.
(His son Menephta led the Reed Sea debacle)
Tutmoses tells how sis Hatshepsut he eschews.
One half-quarried shows slave-production as slaughter.

Flight into Egypt 1949

My six months check of Bible excavations
      Got to Jerusalem and longer heartening stay;
      My hopeful next step: pyramids and Sinai way:
A long war-torn detour ;but United Nations
Had Cairo-planes direct for its delegations
      With sky-view of the Joseph-Mary fate
      In flight from Herod's infanticidal hate.
American pilots secured me reservations.

A lucky break! That same day could begin
      Negotiations for Sinai-trip rare and hard.
Its Greek Orthodox abbot, two months within
      There headed, agreed to take me on as pard.
Meanwhile time for pyramids "step" and "bent";
Luxor and stops for archeologists' dreams meant.

Mummies

An Egypt trademark is its mummies; some
Of common folk, spread quite throughout the world
Museums, or by collectors proud unfurled;
Others still waiting from their graves to come.
But kings apart in Cairo's Museum,
Some dozen Luxor's noblest underworld
Provides; to fame and power in their lifetime hurled:
By skilled embalmers and dry air frail-lifelike become.

Chief is the Seti dynasty: son Ramses Two,
Called Ozymandias, triumphant conqueror;
Likeliest Exodus oppressor of the Jew,
Though son Menephta by Moses was done for,
Phiz still discloses weakness, Ramses strength,
As Tutmoses, who earlier reigned at length.

Adventure: Life

Our life is an adventure ! Who can tell
     What this cute infant someday will become?
     Perhaps a naughty scamp vexing its mum.
Later, sports champ or girl cheerleading yell.
Decision greatest waits: with whom to dwell
     In family love and pangs, cheerful or glum.
     Middle-age success: immense, none, or some ?
In peace or agony or lone, the Reaper's bell ?

Despite resolve and striving, what will be
     Will be; luck undeserved might laggarts crown.
Hard-working talent might disaster see;
     Sometimes the poor leap up, moguls go down.
        Challenge superb and endless: hope and pray
        We may accept serene that final day.

Our Advantageous Differences

Dissimilarities make jolly company !
     Of course, the same-age youngsters flock together,
     And chattiness depends upon the weather.
All kinds it takes to make a world: agree ?
If all were same, how boring it would be !
     Though themes of conversation differ; whether
     One is musician, athlete, or trims leather,
Some things they'll share, enough for repartee.

     Boys won't be girls, but vive la difference !
White/black fit fine in foot/base/basketball.
     Each comment gains its suitable response
When painters, Mormons, docs together fall.
     Then let's be glad we have such ample option,
     Sometimes even ideas suited for adoption

Published in Camillus Good News Nov.2002 p.3

Us as in Camillus

Praise be
That we
So far along life's thorny path have strolled;
Friends past
At last
Have left to us the yellow-brick road of gold.

"Silver Age" some prefer in the euphemism game:
"Golden" having implications of a too-definitive sort.
Most of us still have pep and gutsiness for sport
(TV or real), or for bus-rides adequately short,
Card-games, or singalongs, such livelinesses tame.

This is nothing stealthy;
Exercise is healthy.
A Independence first" some rival institutions claim
As title; and they have a rather forceful point.
"Pay your doctor's bills, then junk his pills"we used to sing
Medics will agree we should do all we may:
Really live while we're alive; there's time later to anoint
Sadly: for now our own activity is just the thing .
Help where it's needed, yes; but firmly toil, rest, or pray

Ah, but that needed help we cannot simply overlook !.
Deeply we owe to all the hundreds every day
Coming from far and wide, in whatever car or bus they took,
Long before dawn or sunshine's earliest ray
Even through rain or blizzard, just to be on time.
Then in the sweltering heat,
Reluctance they defeat!
Others stay on so patiently, until or through the night.
Care-givers all, in such extremely varied specialties,
Cheerful and friendly; glad to lend whatever hand they might

Oft jerked from here to there for unforeseen emergencies;
Pained by worries how best handle food, ills, or grime.

Services numberless are offered, in part to while away
The daylight hours, but oftener for those who would
Improve themselves in something, maybe hand's dexterity,
Puzzles and games or suchlike skills in their own way quite good,
Stitchery, ceramics,
Bingo B nothing panics !
Concerts and lectures on the arts of loftier nobility.
Reading-groups, Classics, who's for Scrabble? or whatever it may
be.
Now and then together to be driven through the Zoo,
Our nearest neighbor; or new lakeside Art Museum too.

Worthy occasions avail for those who feel it's best to pray;
Chapels various invite to preferred rituals every day,
Maybe Catholic chiefly;
Ecumenical some Sundays.
Plus almost any day from Saturdays through Mondays
Chances for exchanging views in a Bible-sharing nation,
Of interest for our Jewish brethren as a treasure held in common
Not unmindful that the Muslims too from it drew inspiration.
Proselytizing no,
But as far as we can go
Helping to make the various inherited faiths a source of peace
And cheerful friendliness, not excluding Manitou or Zen or
shaman.

Remembering that our debt to Saint Camillus cannot cease,
For whom is named the most important hospital in Rome,
While from his sons came impulse for health-service nearer home.
Bless all,
We call,
As we in yellow leaf enjoy the hospitality
Of this so complex project making comfortable and free.

[Abridged p. 97]

Two Rivers

Life is in two ways a river.
     My own life is a winding stream
        (Everyone else's too !)
     Now thunderstruck raising a shiver
With billows disturbingly crashing.
Now gliding placidly plashing
       Or scintillating dew,
     As comfortable as a dream;
Most folks chatter-chatter as their droplets glide
Others prefer a taciturn and thoughtful ride.

Each life-stream is made up of N-billion drops,
     Each a varied experience or positive action.
And future's bewildering change never stops.
Whatever our yearning for peace or distraction.
What we see any moment of life's ongoing flow
       In youth or childhood stage.
       Adulthood or old age,
Is different far from hour, month year, decade ago.
     Yet each life's identity,
      Like the river's, same will ever be.

Not just my life's whole gush like everyone else's
    In what is called the creation
But each single "drop" to which our nature impels us,
    Or life-act in imagination,
Is generally held to be due to one Great Power far above us
    For some an Omnipotent God by this or some other name
Of a Person mysterious able to love us;
    Or called by a few just Nature
    (Or Chemistry, which amounts to the same
    Say scientists; what's in a name ?)
But able to furnish much-needed care to each drop,
    And even quite sate your
Requirements so each River of Life need never derail or stop.
Meanwhile all humankind, N-squared times trillion
Drops of each past or future humanity's billion
    Into a single turbulent stream coalesces,
    Harmonious sometimes, but oftener with distresses
Each for some special advantages struggling madly.
Yet the same Power or Mind to which they owe their existence
Even if via a singular microbe or big Bang, If well or badly,
Wields for each single experience or action of their subsistence
    A fatherlike concern for their proper goal and in-hang.

Such is at least common faith of our three strands
        Of "monotheism Semitic"
            Shared perhaps
        By those with faith in Manitou upgirded,
           Maybe Yin-Yang or Buddhist overlaps,
                Or Zen's "inner peace" unnamed.
        Quarrels of how what we share in belief
           Can most aptly be worded
        Cause and have caused the sad grief
           Of groups at piety aimed
        In struggles atrocious to fall:
        Hence many an intelligent and reasonable critic
           Recoils in horror from any God at all
           Or the very name of Creator,
        Implying for them "bigoted stake-burning hater".

        Yet to "ultimate Power", if person or not,
        All agree can be due
           That stream of each jot
Which looks or acts "anthropic: like people":
        Not "Earthan", though recently only, it's true
        We see Earth as a pinpoint of vast universe
        Maybe with "anthropics"like us, or better or worse.
Without proclaiming "Martians" from the steeple,
        Faith in the River of the created and redeemed
        May face a "manlike" broader than it seemed.

"Power Creating" might care not for just
Carbon compounds with what we call brains
    Possibly quite as much for robust
Weird-looking entirely different strains.
    Whatever the cognate drops,
All together we are in a stream,
    Should not cognates, not slops,
Have peaceful coexistence as our dream?

Proverbs Ten, One sees some "King's mind"
Unifying the wild stream of "like-human"-kind.
    So as we look from bridge or bank
      Of any river, we can see
    Not only the drop to cry out "that's me",
But all the "me-likes" that could live
In union such as "Superpower King" can give.

    So should we either pray
      Or leave all to "Microbe Architect"?
    Hardly !All of us who in some way
      Claim to think can surely suspect
Each must Act, do Something of what
    We can, and not merely stand
With pain for disunity wringing a hand.

No peace amid the nations but
With peace among religions, it is claimed;
        A challenge justified and daring,
        But it seems to imply
We can't effect globe-harmony until we've tamed
Ourselves and our immediate circle to apply
At home self-sacrificing prudent sharing
Such as we would spread afar?
"Save earth for future generations" sounds just fine
But doesn't that remote pretension somewhat jar
        If we're content to underline
Nine-tenths what earth provides is ours or mine?

        Sure, in harmony we long to settle down,
By hungry Third World not envied but admired,
        Helping them with surpluses or renown
Of handouts all unspokenly inspired
        By iron resolve: top dog will always stay
        Our own divinely favored U.S.A.

My life's River is Earth's moat:
An endless web interweaving
    So many streams competing: me,
      My mom and kids; and friends;
There's strangers near or too far to see,
      All with their own concerns.
Most ultimate the Super-Vital Float:
All man-like beings that never ends;
      To our own reasoned free

      Contribution leaving
      Responsibility
That each one's drop will not see others grieving.
"Life a River" is a challenge, not a dream:
      Each competing Me
      Or Group in harmony
Serenely with some adaptation must stream.

Is Poetry-Faith Real?

Poetry-classics quite often and movingly mention
     God as relating to people. If Wordsworth prefers
Baby betraying its soul's immortality, attention
     To the youth-age divine interplay rather Browning refers,
Nor seems concerned with dogma, liturgy, or church.

"Long Easter prayer" leaves Arnold's Merman in lurch.
     Earthier, Arnold cannot will
       "The fire that in the heart resides:
     The Spirit bloweth, and is still;
       In Mystery our soul abides;
         But tasks in hours of insight willed
         Can be through" days of gloom fulfilled.

Poems seem destined not to help a faith's daily needs,
By fostering practice of religion in its variations.
Sin, its forgiveness, laws, sabbath-observance and creeds;
Vestments, incense: archaic other-world relations.
       Almost as if God's role in daily life
       Promoted an against-religion strife.

Dare we ask frankly then "Which seems more fundamental?"
　　　Be a created human? or is to be Christian more attractive?
We now ecumenically admit God is to all gentle,
　　　　Some of his Being revealing to all, and in everyone active.
　　　　　Do poems focus human life more clearly ?
　　　　　Or religious rituals appeal to us more dearly ?

Some question, can't faith bring love and peace among all?
More than religions have done with their bickering fights ?
Not undervaluing which God-aspect should most enthral:
Single out rather for praise what in God reconciles and unites.
　　　　　Is poetry just dream imagination ?
　　　　　Or does it cope with the real-life situation ?

Maybe "To each his own" kind of truce in emergency found:
Helps some more to faith by dispute and zeal for conversion;
Others by dream-vision of God not as warrior but hound
Heavenly, enticing in strange ways to live out his own version.
　　　　　Poetic vision can cooperate
　　　　　Enforcing what all faiths most validate.

Alchemy

This Arab scholars' term
Famed medieval universities
Adopted for their yen to find the germ
Transmuting baser metals into gold:
Ridiculed as academic sophistries,
Yet winning soft poetic mystic hold.

Now after Mendelejeff must we not
Admit that all his "elements" deemed solid
Seem to interchange their subatomic
Particles as whizzing from a pistol shot,
To recombine as entitities not so stolid
Nor subsumed yet in systems economic.

Indeed, the road from substance to components,
Then atom, proton, electron, nuclear sorrow,
Is still an open road, a scholars' midway,
Plenty convincing for what we know today
Not ridiculed by ill-informed opponents,
But waiting a next step to learn tomorrow.

A provisional dream
We might respectfully say;
    An alchemy, it might seem.
All science took off that way.
    Aristotle, Ptolemaeus, Galen
Were not just wrong, but needed
    Ongoing redirection
    At times a real correction.
"Pathfinders" left them not unheeded.
    Rustic guessers got their tale in.

Is not all human life a kind of alchemy,
    Urge to transmute our base stuff into fairer?
Many their wrong-path footsteps do not see;
    But we can profit by their trial and error.

    Alchemy is something like a Holy Grail
A thing to strive our whole life long to find
    A dream which o'er frustrations can prevail
    If others laugh at us, we will not mind;
They laughed at Columbus; he died poor;
    Vexed Galileo, Darwin too from judgment-seat.
But folks will follow ever their dream's lure;
    Many false steps need never mean defeat.

Sacred-Animal Planet

Our four or more footed friends,
    Bible-named, are not holy. But rather
      Conspicuously
    In Leviticus Eleven uncleans gather
      For reasons variously
Claimed hygienic, botanic, or for ends
Mythic; a few experts say
Fascinosum, trembly, is holy some way.
    Unclean means Latin sacra, set apart,
      Like funerals or lawful sex, yes needed
    Yet unearthily touching the heart
      And requiring a ritual well heeded.

      Still and all, "biblical animals"
As title sounds so special and thoughtworthy,
    If we count in the birds and some creepers.
    Like a zoo, it delights yet appalls.
    Noah's Ark saved from an extinction earthy
Though missing some Darwinian sleepers.

First place holds the horse, two hundred times,
  As war's chief weapon of massive destruction;
   Also for its nobility,
   And human mobility;
Man's closest pal: next for us to the dog
In Near East still as then scarce better than hog.
   But for genuine helpfulness, far surpass
   The lowly mule and donkey, called ass:
    For David and Jesus "King's mount",
    But for all as chief burden-carrier count.
     Though camel's lumbering majesty
     Resisted thirst superciliously.

In farmyard then as now there reigned
  Cows and sheep; goats too alas
Whose grazing wrecks all foresting and grass.
   Hebrew Ox meant alike steer or bull
   Even where prohibited to pull
    The plow hitched alongside the ass:
"Mixing the kinds"as with cloth or food pained.

Chickens? No, not one before Peter's cockcrow.
Though quail admittedly kept Exodus on the go.

Eagles abound; some render "vulture's wings".
  Stork's recognized tenderness to her young
Gave us our myth that she our babies brings.
  Swan named; pelican as type of Jesus sung
As parent whose body babe's red beak eats.
Job ostrich harshly, peacock more kindly treats.

Sir Lion, though in rank far behind the horse,
Is "King Predator" though leopard worse.
  Cat, god in Egypt, so in Bible never named.
  Snake for its role in men's death unduly famed.
    Egypt plagues' frog and lice
    Locusts and swarmy flies
     Varyingly shown
     As local nature's own.

     Not one real fish is named
   Though Leviathan and Behemoth are guessed
     And Galilean lake was famed
For apostles' toil; two miracles of Jesus blessed.

Herbarium Sacrum

Plants mentioned in the Bible
Even if not healing
By medievals were liable
To create a sort of feeling
Of sacredness recalling
The miracles enthralling
Of Elijah, Jesus, and some earthgrown herbs:
Whatever the famed "natural order" disturbs.

Cloisters of that all-too believing age
With instinct scientific
Fostered monks' toiling experimental stage
In gardens or in greenhouses prolific
To heal the pains of brothers
And often neighboring others.

But "Flowers of the Bible" nowadays
Comprise weeds, roots, and even trees,
With frequent mention of their healing ways
From aloes, balsam, cummin to the Z's.
Some note Ezekiel's leaves on Jerusalem streams
As only plant called "healing" in Bible reams.

Citing King James with RSV
Corrections, or Greek-Hebrew "proof",
Or rationalizing burning bush, plagues, manna,
And palms of the Hosanna,
Coping with claimed implausibility
With scholarly intention, not in spoof.

Yet taking Magdalen's Risen-Jesus-Gardener in stride,
Inculcates for nature's beauty more concern,
Cutting through Bible-terms a swathe quite wide
In hopes that we some real facts may learn.

"Rose", though called lily, never occurs
Unless as the shoshan generic;
Rose of Jericho or Sharon still more errs
For hyacinth or tulip esoteric.

But quite correct are onion/garlic so missed
In fleeing Egypt, though manna was insect-dropping.
Palm is from Herodotus to Linnaeus kissed
As tree all others overtopping.

Yet brambles King of Trees were able
To be named in Judges Nine fable.
Thorns are classed with noxious plants or dyes,
And spices Solomon's India fleet prize.
Mandrake as Viagra for Rachel served,
As benzedrine for Greeks, Mid-Age anesthetic.
Moses' bulrush to paper-stuff was swerved;
Vine as ever appealing and pathetic.

Olive and oil made a valued streak
Of Mediterranean lands mid-level,

Equated with the origins of Greek
And Latin culture where Bible-diffusions revel.

Almond was"watcher"in Jeremy's first chapter.
Apple was really apricot; maybe its coloring
Gave Tappuach in modern Hebrew adapter
For orange Tappuz, gold-apple-like thing.

Hummus a kind of peanut-butter from chickpea;
Cedar of Lebanon Bible's noblest tree.
Frankincense/myrrh were clue to India trade
Lentils a trap for hungry Jacob made.

To Zacheus's sycamore belong
Chances for what is called Jesus' only humor,
Why did he curse the fig that did no wrong?
Its poultices helped Hezekiah, is the rumor.

Thankfully we acclaim
All plants, whate'er the name!

Amerindian Prayer

A missionary enterprise
Diffused as prayerful Indian talk:
"Great Spirit, help me never criticise
My neighbor, till I walk
In his moccasins a mile".

Truly a thoughtful reflection,
Perhaps reminding us of "I complained I had
No shoes, till toward me crawled a lad
With no feet"; or a similar connection:
"What would I have done if I were in
His shoes?" ere taxing anyone with sin.

But that an Indian "said a prayer"
Did not fit with what little I'd learned
On the shape of our Indians' devotion;
Though I doubt not the man was aware,
Of the "skyey Beings" and priests who turned
Braves' thoughts up with feasts and emotion.

Plural "Beings" to us is an unsettling view
But "Heavenly Ones" is much closer
To our "Heaven only knows" or Thank Heaven!
From respect, not thinking of Trinity, true.
Maybe the Indian thought "Skies"
Collective, since like us,
He could not realize
What God exactly was.

Their numerous highly honored "Priests"
Were really Medicine-Men: they dispose
Of liturgies and amulets believed
To put them best in contact by their many
feasts
With the Transcendent, specially when arose
Challenges to the braveries they achieved.

In this background, some may have said "a prayer"
But such religiosity in their tradition
Was not so prominent as in the Christian.
Yet both showed a faith equally aware
Of what our prayer-manuals call
"Presence of God": for us too, base of all.

Arab Free(-ing) Verse
[A. Hourani, History of the Arab Peoples (Harvard 1991) 396; 444]

Iraqi Sayyab of Jaykur claimed
  Villagers streaming into cities means
  A new world; a new poetic language weans.
Rhyme-meter vanish, at new symbols aimed.

  French, English, and Islamic,
Even Eliot's Greek Adonis symols subsume
  Into a startlingly updated poetry-dynamic,
A new Arab poetics to illume.

Not like traditional poetry read to mobs familiar;
  Arcane, yet expressing their growing malaise;
   If Islamic, yet not Azhar-style;
Rather with social-justice aims peculiar:
   "Men for others" Qor'an seems to profile
   Sometimes hinting even what Marx says.

Meanwhile paramount became the "Nation",
    Pan-Arab nationalism, claimed new Syria
      Baath-"Resurrection" party.
      Christian Aflaq its vocal smartie.
Others hailed a worldwide Islamic integration
    Forming a nationality superior.

      A third strong trend
      Was to defend
Colonial French-British borders,
Within which local elite families had power
    And populace submitted to their orders.
            It was the hour
Of nationalisms imbedded in a shower
    Of manifold and hostile nations
    All Arab, all Islamic, but in odd relations.

      A fourth force looms
To claim the freed-verse voice:
    Not Marxists or anarchists alone,
But all-surpassing Economics choice
Of Secularism as only valid ruling throne
Upheld by distaste for sectarian religious glooms.

Few contemporary poets reject
Islam entirely, but many
Advocate "redimension" with respect.
Some praise religion as an inherited culture,
Thus humanistic, prey to criticism, and any
Who find it antisocial may give it up;
"Muslim Brothers" retain Qor'an as God's lineup
But for Mecca times, to be updated at a venture
To fit the needs. As Christians say,
And changing language of today.

We must take history into account
To exploit possession of our past,
Yet recognize it's not a fixed amount,
But goal-aimed to become our future at long last.
Wile other Muslim Brothers claim Sahria,
Qoranic "Law" alone and undiluted
Gives still today, as in Iran,
And in the North-Sudan
Fundamentalist restructuring all by West polluted.
Thus free verse gets ever noisier and freer.

Eliot and Pound

Lifelong friends, stern mutual-critic editors,
  Universally agreed to be
  Last century's greatest poets, especially
In influence on dawning poet-meteors:
  And thus by some at least
  Held daystars of the feast
  Of Free Verse, which conditions
That century's entire U.S. production
Of previously metered and rhymed construction
  Displacing six centuries of traditions.

  Both expatriates by choice,
  Otherwise unlike:
  Britain gave T.S. Eliot voice
  But tempted Ezra Pound's dislike,
Who throve in France and mostly Italy;
  Favoring Fascist and Nazi economic,
By America deemed unstable criminally.
  Eliot moderate, conciliating, rarely comic.
  St. Louis boy, of Washington U. founder
  Firm Unitarian minister a sprout;
Harvard- and Joyce Ulysses-trained astounder,
Then British citizen and Anglican devout.

From then date Eliot's Ash Wednesday, Magi,
  With few random or capricious rhymes;
   Real rhymed couplet rows shove
   Into rare Tempter or Four Knights of
Becket's Cathedral Murder impassioned, wry.
   Patron of Free Verse more in later times'
Experiments with choruses in Christian Rock.
His earlier Waste Land still is his peacock.
I heard him read in Roman College jam-packed hall
Verses, with famed "not bang but whimper", I recall.
   His use of rhyme quite limited remains
   To earliest Prufrock and 14 Cat refrains.

   Pound's virtually only work
Was a colossal epic of some hundred Cantos
   Modifying or worsening traits that lurk
In his Cathay, Propertius, Mauberley romantos.
    His aim: to square the circle
    Uniting skills incompatible:
    A new "sailing after knowledge" Odyssey,
    Wherever one could go, curious and free:
Poet, translator, historian of troubadour lyric
    And of Confucius China governments
    And earliest U.S. presidents,
Chemistry, economics: a victory pyrrhic.
    Imagining he could provide
Unified understanding to bewildered men
    Of all that Science and scholarship let slide
     Into their ken.

To understand anyone's poem, it's been said,
    It must be memorized and declaimed aloud;
And that's how schoolchildren are well led
    To appreciate the classic verse hailed proud.
      For Hopkins' sonnets there's no other way
      To grasp their sense and unity.
    This applies to Eliot's Waste Land, say,
      Or easier snatches of Pound's apogee.
    Random disconnected flashes
        Of Free Verse take on sense
    When silently-read plashes
Might tempt to mutter just "nonsense".

    Critics of Free Verse variously claim
Its success due to "America must rank on high"
    Or "Our Science era teaches us to aim
Anything experimental and new to try".
    Whatever be the Why, the fact is clear:
    Disciplined rhyme has yielded to new condition.
    "Public acceptance" norm which made so dear
    6 (really 26) centuries of verse-tradition
Now must demand a fair-play hearing
For Eliot-Pound schools, without jeering.

Are our "Gifts" Free ?

We, by terrorists berated,
By our bankers and vote-seekers stated
As wildly generous, yet slated
For attack by those most fated
    To Third World grinding poverty
    Reply calmly: "Can't they see
    We are doing what can be,
    And they react so enviously ?"
But Islam and Europeans judge us harshly and reply:

    "You send leftovers and scraps,
    Or strange foodstuffs which perhaps
    Drop wealth in your farmers' laps,
    Or are ultimately traps,
        Treat receivers as your vassal,
        Threat 'withholding' if they hassle,
        Think a decorative tassle
        Hides what any starving mass 'll
Recognize as your maneuvers to keep powerholders high."

Yes, our TV and computers
    And inventive pharmaceuters
Have immensely helped mud-rooters
Despite rebels and far-shooters;
        But our unions and lawmakers
        Frankly claim there'll be no takers
        Among competition-makers:
    All must pay our banker-slakers
In prices which for starving economics meet the sky.

Export-import legislation
Is controlled by this rich nation
Despite foreign agitation
To our sole gain and elation:
        "Yes, we'll help on one condition"
        (So lawmakers see their mission)
        "That no foreign competition
    Or price-adjusting manumission
Our folk's over affluent comfort lessens by a jot; don't let
                                                them try."

But what up on one pan goes
Must as simple weighing shows
Go as every grocer knows
Down the other: shafts disclose.
        We must accept some loss
        By the economic toss.
        Just to show that we are boss
        We must obey the market's laws.
Hundred percent equality; no! but improvement, do or die.

[Abridgment of p.71 above]

The Twin River

Life's stream is a river that to each can deliver
Now placidly plashing, now vividly splashing,
Then thunderously crashing as if planning stops.
For some it chatter-chatters as it flows,
For others thoughtful-taciturnly goes.

Not just my own life's streams of N-billion drops, it seems,
But the cumulated gleams of each life that ever was,
N-squared trillion drops conflation, life-acts in imagination,
Of what is called creation, meaning what the Great Power does,
Guiding each one's drops with concern that never stops,
Father-like, called "Microbe-Architect" by chemists tops.

Whether "personal Creator" or name dear to Christian-hater
To his products never traitor source of all our being guides.
Whatever is "anthropic", human-like both furred and tropic,
Not just "Earthan", maybe Martian or not even carbon-prides.
Possibly weird-looking wholly non-conformist strains,
"Life" (like God's!) means not just functioning with brains.

When we gaze from bank or bridges at a flow shoving its ridges
We may fancy "Life Whatever" cognate drops within a stream:
One strand twisting, 'Why, that's me" we recognize exultingly,
But look again ! we see everything anthropic in our dream.
Should not peaceful coexistence with them all be our fond hope ?
Not "Star-wars" or heretic-burners; the rest fall within our scope.

My Girl-Friend

When age ten and in grade eight, I somehow felt it was my fate
Like older mates to have a girl, take her books, walk her from school.
She accepted my advances, though we never went to dances,
Just to movies and the Fair, valentines and gifts the rule.

Then came day of graduatin', "fare thee well" and off to Creighton;
Soon novitiate was my fickle passion; I thought of her no more.
Till one day in Rome my phone said a girl awaited lone
Down in glass-framed parlors where we safe could close the door.

She just said "I'm Nora's daughter" and my innards turned to water,
Fearing that some shyster lawyer sent to sue for DNA paternity!
Not at all! just mom's new surname, of course same as her name,
And we chatted pleasantly of days that I was never more to see.

Mom had heard I now was centered in Rome where all roads entered,
And had asked her as a tourist there to greet me; she could try.
"Thanks to Mom for--pityingly--taking my preposterous gallantry",
I said (she was pretty) "and I'm glad she found a so much better guy"

Rediscovering Assyria

Like Bush, I found Iraq quite cruel when I went east fresh from school
To verify if our archeology was the real state of things
"No visa for passport that has one from Israel" came the snort.
A month I spent in Beirut while in Baghdad friends pulled strings.

Finally got it; then Berlin-Baghdad train to Jonah's Nineveh plain;
They call it Mosul, whence named Mussolini and the muslin strands.
Then a local in vexation left me off at desert station;
Curled up there till dawn, due east on foot cross desert sands.

After two miles desolation and almost in desperation
I saw two donkeys bearing man and woman with my horizon blend;
The man, courteous, said"Welcome, stranger, now you gladly shall come
On that donkey", whence he bade his loving wife descend.

"Oh I couldn't; where I'm from 'Ladies First' is rule-of-thumb!"
"Then take mine" and down he jumped , but winked her off to let him ride.
Famed pre-Christmas painting: Joseph walks, rides Mary Queen
Sans account of mid-east customs where of course the girl will stride.

At Assur I started prowling, quick arrested by cop growling:
Angry commandant warned my throat might for my Rolex have been slit;
Then assigned a young detective as my guide and spy protective,
To climb the ziggurat and look around a little bit.

Sent me in jeep to midnight train; off at Baghdad, past all pain
In the U.S.-Jesuit college, now long banned as tyrant-warden.
Then to Babylon so famed, but with its Babel-tower just named
And on to Ur and Persian Gulf and by desert bus all night to Jordan.

Archeological Apologetics

Outset of Palestine excavation aimed to promote people's salvation
When from almost every nation priests and Bible-teachers strove
With all their righteous might to prove the Scriptures right
By bringing up to sight what centuries there throve.

1800 thereabout Rosetta Stone from Delta out
Trilingual came to rout ignorance of old Egyptian tongue,
Pharaoh histories past count. Then from Behistun the fount
Trilingual for a vast amount of Akkadian lore from desert sprung.

Pre-Genesis millennium Enuma Elish creation-sum
And Gilgamesh with plum of a Noah's Ark with Flood.
Faith was menaced with suspicion, but the Church now saw its mission
In Palestine: transmission of like documents to bud.

Zounds ! not one was found, only scribbled scraps abound
With bible-names background much less frequent than today.
Scholars' goal now became not to prove a given fame
But to figure how so same yet different from what Iraq had to say.

And to weigh the picture-writing of Egyptian tombs; the fighting
Of polytheist-priests inciting mobs against new monotheist king.
And portrayals of future life: first "confessing" not sins rife
But sinlessness and strife against every weird-god fling.

Faith apart, what was the history winding through the Bible-mystery?
What Pharaoh hit-or-miss story of the Joseph/Moses gambles?
Did Abram's clan really roam from Ur or Harran to Canaanite home ?
Or was one tribe's palindrome symbol of some unifying scrambles?

So for a century scholars move God's Word to clarify, not prove;
But now some disapprove: say what archeology has shown
Is that every Bible act is a record not of fact
But of campfire-stories backed by belief-traditions lone.

Experts hitherto compared Bible-histories and shared
This or that detail bewared, but now there dimly looms
Upon our horizon claim "Israel's history" is just a game
To keep believers tame amid excavation's glooms.

Paul's Footsteps in Turkey

"Ramsay's", we might rather say;
For that nineteenth-century ray
Lights and guides us still today,
    Since no other pioneer
Followed through Acts' interven-
    ing obscurer steps, between
Tarsus dig and Ephesus, seen
    Exegetes to domineer.

    Outset "Syrian Antioch",
Now within the Turkish block
And by them re-named "Antak-
ya" (scarce a trace of Peter there).
    But from its Seleucia port
    Paul with varying escort
    Set sail Christ to transport
In Rome's empire everywhere.

    Via a Yalva -Antioch, "near"
Not "in" Pisidia, he'll appear
Excavated some miles rear
    Of its thriving modern town.
I met an ancient sire inside,
Who had been Sir Ramsay's guide,
    And chatted with glad pride
Of their explorings of renown.

    On to Lystra; known as "twin
    Roman colony" it had been
Inscribed on a sherd found in
    Town south of Iconium.

Derbe, site more in dispute,
Was the last stop in Paul's route
Thence back via Antioch to scoot
To Antalya port to come.
Near Perga was that port,
Hard to reach by present sort
Of Turkish bus-transport;
I arrived there at midnight.
Word got quick around the stop:
"American aboard !so hop
And bring the 'Koreli'", tip-top
Ally of our Korean fight.

They dragged him from his bed
And his smile to all quick spread
As from his weary head
He pulled some Yankee gab as if 'twas fun.
Yes, in Turkey hinterland
Then a Yank was special, and
It assured a welcome grand
Like Paul's "I'm Roman citizen !"

Trip Two: with partners changed
Paul a longer route arranged;
But in passing Derbe, ranged
Timothy for office new.
In New Troy Paul had a dream
Calling him his faith to beam
Into Europe, with esteem
For Athenians and Corinth too.

From Corinth, Ephesus just briefly;
Then Jerusalem of our belief he

Visited while planning chiefly
A third tour back to Ephesus.
There the silversmiths' uproar
About "Diana evermore !"
Then quietly up the shore
To Macedon to end the fuss.
Upon returning with a stop
At New Troy again to shop
For converts with non-stop
Fervent third-floor midnight talk
So long a boy on window-sill
Dozed and fell out to his ill.
All rushed down."It didn't kill !"
Cried Paul, enabling him to walk.

Then past Lesbos isle by boat,
Past Ephesus too to float
To Miletus, lump in throat,
For Ephesians' sad farewell.
Sailing on to Rhodes and Tyre;
At Caesarea landing dire
Thence to face Jerusalem's ire
And his conversion-tale retell.

Smaller Turkish towns we'd touch
(Paul, Ramsay, me, and such)
Enjoying very much
Some Roman/Byzantine remains.
Also Tarsus birthplace-site,
Excavated as is right;
Bumping anywhere with delight
Into hints of Pauline gains.

Growing Old Gracefully

"Grow old along with me;
The best is yet to be"
Said Browning; yet could he
Claim thus early to foresee
What a same-yet-different aging
Year 2004 is staging :
Sex and secularism raging;
Where's two-parent family!

Living in a hospice care
Has advantages; we share
Our miseries, and thus some spare
And can't on the others blame.
The caregivers are tops,
And save us futile stops
Or topplings, and serve delicacies worth the name.

Though deaf, I'm quite a talker:
Some would say a noisy squawker;
And I ought to use a walker,
Though I much prefer my cane.

My stern asthma medication
Scheduled with regimentation
Is as pesky as tarnation;
And night's sleep can be a bane,

Luckier perhaps are those
Who in daughter's home can close
Their counts, with one who knows,
Can call quick aid when crises mar.

Visits from the darling small,
Grand-nieces cute or nephews tall.
Some who take you to the Mall,
Or just sightseeing in their car.

Now we have time for reflection
On life's meaning, and selection
Of pursuits as now best section
Of our sedentary state.
Even not with pristine skill,
Just for company or to kill
Time, we play cards, singalong, or thrill
At TV or books our spirits to elate.

All in all, if not life's best,
Age gives meaning to the rest.
We can face each day with zest,
Readying for that final call.
With some prayers but not of terror
And some hopes of which they're bearer,
And expectation no scarer
Of a future far from small.

Fearless then let's summon age
To concede youth's heritage!
Young, all was vague and rag-
ing; we shall know, being old.
We agree the Potter's hand
Perfects now the cup as planned:
Not just by paradox they scanned
Our years as "the Age of Gold".

Artsies Born Not Made

Child-prodigy musician owes much to the technician
Skilled in musicality in his genes or family.
      Look at Mozart, Hopkins, or your choice.
Artsy-craftsy types as well owe to genes more than they tell,
School, pals, and inclination help, but less, eventuation.
      The skill that's in our parents will find voice.

Maybe all in all it's better Nature bears out to the letter
A Kids religion get from ma, politics and sport from pa";
      Though sex-roles seem lately up for grabs.
The hundred lads or lasses quite devout in home or classes,
Maybe hundred dandy pitchers, home-run kings, voter-bewitchers
      Fit real life better than the one who strums or dabs.

But if culture's to continue, some few have to get the venue
The fine arts to cultivate or machines to actuate
      Or invent ones needed by technology.
School or home, at three or five they must start if to survive:
The paint-brush or violin, monkey wrench or silo-bin
      Need attention and support from infancy.

Not rash cloning DNA; genes themselves will have their say
In putting at our service talents rare that make folks nervous
      But are truly human, effort worth and sacrifice,
So parents, pastors, teachers, keep eyes peeled for those features
Which if fostered culminate in genius needed, rare, and great.
      Scarcely less than prayers or baseball worth the price.

Advertising for job-seekers of eighteen as skylight-streakers
For the fine arts or the latest technology advances greatest
      (Entertainment world draws millions: off the point).
It's too late; they must be sought where and when the genes have brought
And families have fostered in the hope they will have prospered
Artsy-craftsy gifts are treasures you can't find at any joint!

Stocks plummet, investors gain !?

This improbable headline crept in before the deadline
Of a "Socially Responsible Investing" flyer titled In All Things.
But its theme deserves a hearing: not "financially endearing"
Is the only value which frm ethical investment springs.
       Take a look what else it brings!

To reduce to quotient/number is not easy, heavy lumber,
In assigning to improvement of the near community,
Roles played by wise investing, or in clean environment questing,
Or in salvaging effectively true values of democracy.
       "Money talks" and so do stocks, we see.

Investment means supporting some CEO's deporting
Of the firm to which it furnishes an operating base.
Can any social-minded investor be so blinded
As not to see his profit help some unjust profit-pace
       That was not his own aim in the race.

While apartheid was the top fight, once in priestly garb at stop-light
On Marquette campus I was challenged by a total stranger:
"Why don't you", he sneered, "divest?"; garb and site supplied the rest.
He was claiming Church supported social evils by the danger
       Of stockholding in some South Africa arranger !

But now the experts say divesting is a coward's way
Of escaping a responsibility he could struggle for instead
Two-thousand "advocacy" hold gives the right to be so bold
As to vote by proxy "No" to evil-smelling moves he sees ahead.
       One small part-owner raised his head !

"Non-profit" groups need millions, so investment aims toward billions,
For functioning of hospitals, churches, universities.
But investment for increasing needed funds requires no ceasing
In their proxy struggle for their social justice pleas.
       That's the gain our title sees.

Arche- (?Anthrop-) ology

A most important big
Bible-related dig
With walls aplenty at Jericho excavated
In "Archeology
And Anthropology
Annals" was published and updated.

Except for "Classical"
And later "Biblical"
World-archeology is usually seen
Chiefly as a source
And often only course
For anthropology, old culture's queen.

The "Classical" suggests
Greek-Roman sculpture quests
Like Elgin, and the Vatican Laocoön;
And humbler artifacts
Mid which their background acts:
Life-styles European culture rests upon.

World-archeology evokes
Aztecs or Polynesian folks
For traits to anthropology most pertaining;
Recently these can seem
Historians' only gleam
To fill their blanks in long-past lives explaining.

"Why not for Palestine too ?
Earth-yielded source will do
For writing history, objective and without
That tinge of faith, which blurs
Bible-based histories". demurs
The odd "ex-biblical excavator" scout.

We know and must admit
It was for Holy Writ
To "prove it true" such digging first began.
Apologetic stance,
Bordering on romance,
Quickly reworded to "show its background" plan.

But this was background which
Turned out to be so rich
It took over as the tail that wagged the dog.
Genesis-creation and the Ark
Of Noah really hark
Back to imitating tales from Babylonian bog

Churchmen agreed, revising
Millennial emphasizing
Of God's word-choice to spokesmen on their own
In Jonah fish story too
And standstill-sun review:
Like Jesus' parables, need not historical fact clone.

And yet there is a thread
Abram to Ezra, led
Through telling of a story not proved wrong.
No such history-hints at all
Can artifacts recall

Where no Egypt-Iraq style documents throng.

Bible-interests remain
To justify the pain
And cost of digging for so slight a crop
More anthropology
Than usable history:
Insights to rescue exegetes from total flop.

Homer-Kudos

During my college late-teens all my days, even nights were expended
Reading and parsing my Homer, weirds to normal Greek amended;
Also comparing with Plato and Sophocles, New Testament, Pindar,
Rich as a source of our culture, which sheer pleasure too did not hinder.

Then fate transferred me to Biblical teaching and tours; toward a new star:
Babylon, Egypt, and Hebrew research, all to Greek near yet too far.
Sixty years later retired, relaxation I found in light reading
Westerns, best-sellers, Victorian, poetry too not impeding.

Surfeited finally, "Why not a bit try Homer again?" I reflected,
"Since we have luckily fine Loeb Greek-English editions perfected".
Challenged Ulysses-like now by such elderly struggles and wanderings,
Maybe rewarding withal, ran my octogenarian ponderings.

What a surprise was awaiting, as the Greek words slid by me so musical
Or were familiar from everyday medico-pharmaceutical.
Homer made everything easy by throwing in plenty of"fillers",
Formulas, role-holders too as in paperback modern-day thrillers.

'Ox-eyed Athena','the homeward-return day', and 'Dawn rosy-fingered';
'Far their dear fatherland' ever 'near sounding seashore they lingered'.
Oh how these phrases so pleasantly carry our classical reading along
Save when notorious similes with farm, hunt, or fishing terms throng.

Tales exploding with brief Attic terms or some sputtering oddment
In which two or three of the letters suffice to recall what the god meant.
Breath-taking exploits of Hector with goddesses cruel interfering.
When will Achilles leap back from his pouting aloof longtime jeering ?

How while scarce coping with Homer's caprice and mystique at eighteen
Could I the pleasure thus stored up for seventy years have foreseen?
Not for so many, it's true, can linguistics entice more than sport,
But for the few who are called it can make a long lifetime seem short!

Australian ('Strine') Outback and In

First named the "Southerly-Wind -- australis -- Spirit-of-God land",
Like U.S. Georgia deemed lonely and suited to prisoner-trod land,
Mightily though soon developing its broad southeast corner
Into a world-power inside which no English-speaker felt foreigner.

Those so-called "convicts", few murderers or bank-robbers, rather
Guilty of six hundred "crimes": grabbing hankies or what starvers could gather,
Plus some thousands "transported" for being (North-) Irish wrong-ended:
All-in-all citizenry turning out just as solid as nature intended.

"Outback" is called the northwestern two-thirds of the nation
Sort of retreat for bewildered aboriginal population.
Utterly unlike New Zealand's loud-shouting resistant Maoris:
Shrinking away from white penalties, justice, mercy, and glories.

Hard it is to meet up with some primitive tribal survivals
From the unknown but diverse directions onetime first arrivals;
Lepers in hospice (ex-Jesuit) far north, west of Darwin today claim
Dozens, but rather assimilated now, thus friends and okay tame.

Some with their products are shown off in Sydney as in a museum,
Like the sadly inert kangaroos in the zoo you can see 'em.
Roam the whole outback from Alice to Perth, you'll scarce see some
Blacks or marsupials real, and both timidly visitors flee from.

Cities of course are quite gorgeous, with immigrants most European
Spanking Australian Encyclopedia accounts for all you've been seein':
Church-growth impressive: Anglican, Mormon, Rome motivation;
Culture "down under" unique, well worth tourists' investigation.

Midsummer beaches so sunny at Christmas are hard to get used to,
Chilliest season and school-term July is for us an abuse too.
Northerners gape in amaze: Southern Cross in the night sky !
Always some "Strines" are enchanted with Transiberian "Rilewye".

Homer's Sci-Fi Robots
Translation of Iliad 18,410-422

Vulcan-Hephaestus, great god of his dark underworldly smithy,
Rose from his anvil-stumps upward, a burly gigantic; therewith he
Showed his sad lameness, but both his dwarfed legs bore him on unimpeded.
Bellows-row dragged he away from the fire; other tools his toil needed
Threw he inside of a silvery box, as his face he was sponging,
Wiping both hands; and to dry stubby neck and chest lunging;
Flung on a shirt, seized his sturdiest cane, and got safe to the doorway
Limping; but lo ! on each side there rose up from the floorway
Golden maids, figurative? no: but bright metal casings just like two real girls
Moving in to support their creator and lord, who within them unfurls
Mind fully able to think and to feel; voice-box too that can chatter;
Physical strength and the skill to transform into artifacts matter:
Gift of the gods; thus they offered to help, but he quite on his own power
Reels to where Thetis, Achilles' god-mother awaits on her throne-dower.

Achilles' Panchromatic Shield

"Shield of Achilles" unnumbered the books or short articles named in
Internet sources or library catalogues, equally famed in
Greek-centered cultural circles, without any slightest relation
Factually to the real Iliad book 18, or a translation,
Chapman's or Pope's, or more erudite footnote-edition.
Name has become just a symbol of classic or political condition.
Pity ! because that brief passage itself is a marvelous token,
Showing the skill and variety past praise for which Homer is spoken,

Iliad 18, 468-608 translated
I.City of feasting and litigation, 477-508

Favor to Thetis' Achilles: Hephaestus quick limped to his bellows
Fronting the fire, bade to its job along with its fellows:
Twenty together they blew on the underground smelters
From every direction a well-flaming blast each one pelters:
Sometimes to function along with his toil, but sometimes again
Waiting for beck of Hephaestus to hustle the toil of his den.

Into the fire he flung the resistant raw copper and tin too,
Precious gold as well and silver the melt he threw into.
Then his next step was to shove a giant anvil onto its holder,
Grasping in one hand a hammer, made the other a fire-tongs enfolder

First then creating the Shield, thing gigantic and firmly resistant,
Every inch skillful he wrought, put a shining rim round it insistent,
Glittering in three layers, attached to a silver-made sling-strap.
Five were the folds of the Shield itself; on the outermost wing-flap
Space for the many intaglios to be shaped with masterly cunning.

Background: earth's surface and sky and waters o'errunning,
Sun ever toilingly bright, yet with glimpse of the full moon's own rays,
Star-formations as well with which dark skies are crowned in their own ways:
English names just as Greek: Pleiades, Hyades, strong Orion,
Arctic, the "Bear" of the Pole, north star in the Dipper or Wagon, night-sky in:
Circling about and pointing Orion always in plain view
Never to sink below Ocean-bath Grecian horizons of yore as remain new.

Tale of two cities of mortals like Merops he wove on the metal.
Beautiful towns; in one was a wedding festivity fair as a petal.
Brides from the nuptial chambers, bright with the torches all blazing
People paraded through town, their song hymeneal upraising.
Youths in and out in their nimble-foot dancing whirled, as among them
Clarinet-flutes with lyres vying so musical almost outsung them.
Ladies in wonderment charmed stood riveted each to her doorstep.

Not all was joy; in the agora milling crowds angrily sore step:
Struggle shown rising; two men over blood-price payment disputing,

Claiming he could or did pay it; the other intent to deny
This case was such where a payment did or indeed could apply.
Both are shown keen upon adjudicator's decision awaited;
Mob favor's applause for the one or the other storms up unabated.
Heralds are seen holding crowds back, while elders respected
Sitting in polished bright stones' holy circuit the data inspected,
Holding in hand the loud heralds' authority-scepters
But springing up one by one like jurors proclaiming accepters:
There in the midst lie two talents so gleamingly golden
Payable only to him whose claim would be firmly upholden.

II. City Besieged in War, 18,509-540

Meanwhile surrounding another fair town are shown gleaming in armor
Two military battalions debating two plans how to harm her:
Sack her entire? or by treaty half the riches take over
Gorgeous as such a fort city holds; but they'd soon discover,
"No!' to capitulation; armed in ambush instead, all decided;
Spouses and children along the high walls to defend them abided,
With them the elders good-willed but no longer so spry for attacking;
Fitter ones dug in with Ares' and Pallas Athena's strong backing:
Both shown figured in gold and clad in gold garments
Larger than life and more splendid than soldiers or varmints:
Just as befits the divine, conspicuous; mortals quite dwarfing

To a spot they judged suited for ambush resisters rushed scoffing:
Riverside watering-place for whatever alive that needs drinking;
There they sat safe in their sparkling bronze, they were thinking.
Problem would be all those cattle: a couple of scouts are glimpsed peering.
Quick came the warning of beasts, two herders with them in the clearing,
Leaping up, all of the ambushing warriors, at sight of the stranger,
Piping an innocent pastoral song, unaware of their danger.
Cut pathways to stampede off the cattle and then more easily scattered
Flocks of the woolly white sheep, but the herders to cruel death were battered.

Noticing moos of the cows, the besiegers broke off the debating
In their assembly, and hastily rushed to their horses, berating
Sloth of attack, but their high-prancing steeds quickly brought them
Riverbed-level to line up confronting foes, any who sought them.
Both took their stand at the riverbanks, each near a brother;
All aimed their brazen-tip spears and relentlessly struck one another.

Goddesses "Strife" and "Uproar" quickly joined them, and Fate the destroyer.
She pulled forth one living just wounded; a second unharmed, an annoyer;
Dead was a third whom she dragged by the feet through the tumult; both shoulders
Wearing a shawl freshly reddened with blood of the struggling soldiers.
Joined in are shown all three mixing and fighting like mortals,
Dragging away the bodies of many just flung through death's portals.

V. Royal Farmland, 18,541-560

Then the smith edgeward contrived soft rich soil new-ready for farming,
Broad and thrice-turned, but still plowmen upon it in number alarming
Twisted their teams up and back, digging now and again a new furrow.
Every time they turned back and arrived at their starting-point burrow,
Someone is shown handing over to them honeyed wine in a beaker.
Fortified thus and refreshed they return to their swathe ever sleeker,
Not for preeminence, only for finishing off their so toilsome round.
Black to the rear of them shown every clod of the turned-over ground --
Marvel of marvels ! though this part was gold as the scenery around..

Next was a regal terrain-holding shown with its harvesting reapers.
Wheat-sickles sharp in industrious hands, and quite near were the heapers:
Many the handfuls that cover the swathe as the reaping progresses.
Several laborers twisting the straw to hold bundles in tresses.
Three of the twisters stood waiting, as youngsters behind them
Grab in arms sheaves of wheat as they fall, pass to those who should bind them:
Ever more armfuls they furnish. The King there among them reflective,
Holding his scepter is glad at a yield in no way defective.
Heralds apart are seen under an oak making ready a meal
Busy with carving an ox they have butchered; meanwhile a real
Crowd of the women are sprinkling some barley for tastier dinner.

IV. Vineyard and Ranch, 18,561-589

Nor was there lacking a bountiful vineyard, each cluster a winner.
Background was shiningly golden, but grapes were all indigo somehow;
Silver however the posts along stringing vines hued brown-plum now.
Bluish around flowed a moat all encircled with tin-fence formation
Bridged with but one single path for the carriers each in due station,
Vintagers there back and forth passing, footfalls all firm and not nervous,
Girlish and boyish were all, delighted --enjoying the service,
Baskets of wicker filled up with sweet-ripened fruits they were bringing.

Full in their midst was a lad with a clear-sounding cithara singing
Passionately the famed Linus-song, chant with a delicate ringing
Softly soprano; the hearers in unison stamping their feet ever plainer,
Jubilant, skippingly keen to accompany their young entertainer.

Space was filled out by many an ox with horns long yet straight too
Herded, and shown in a golden and tin-shined formational plate you
Praise, yet detect they are rushing from dungyard to pasture with bellows
Past a resounding swift river, toward swaying rushes in yellows.
Golden were also the cowpokes; just four with the cattle were striding;
White partly were nine alert and swift footed dogs with them gliding.
Wait ! two horrible lions sneaked in with the front rows of cattle,
Dragged in their grasp a strong howlingly bellowing bull in fierce
battle
After them hustled the dogs, with them all the youths fast pursuing
Nevertheless the beasts tore the great bull's hide off and were chewing
Innards and gulping down black-looking blood, though the herders
Strove to sick forward the dogs; these were swift, but fearing their murders
Hung back and naturally turned away from outright attacking
Lions starving; they bravely stood barking loudly but real courage lacking.
Not far the famed doubly-lame smith wrought a pasture, green meant he.
Opening in a ravine, itself ample with white sheep aplenty,
Sheepfolds too, with thatched huts, and shelters for grievement.

V Dance, 18,590-608

Handicapped, yet could the artist frame off his achievement:
Cunningly shows village-green just like the grand one in Knossos
Daedalus made for his tressed Ariadne, footfall-soft with its mosses.
Many the youths there with top-value quality maidens were dancing,
Linking their hands with each other, clasped wrists in their prancing.
Girls mostly gowned in soft sparkling linen, but boys garbed in tunic
Woven enchantingly, soft-oiled and glistening, not like any eunuch.
Bright coronets girls wore, men gold swords with silver-straps hanging.
All were cavorting entrancingly, nimble feet wistfully banging,
Planning their moves like vase-maker with wheel in hand whanging.
Then at times gathered in disciplined rows all lined up together.
Crowds wandered cheering around enjoying the dance and fine weather.
Two clever acrobats also were mingled among them, performing,
Taking the lead for the singers and dancers in melody storming.

Outermost rim of the clever and strongly-made Shield:
Ocean's great might was installed drinking in rivers' yield.

MEMORY LANE ODE

1. OMAHA (1916-) 1920-1931

My life began in Iowa City realm of university,
    They say; I don't remember, nor Charleston S.C.,
Where Mom for want of anything to do
    Awaiting Navy dad's return from France
Taught me to read at three they say or maybe two.
    Still Iowa, his birthplace Cherokee a memory by chance.
        Then quick to practice law
        In nearby Omaha
    Near cousins in the suburb called Dundee.

To build a new St. Margaret Mary's school
    The Mercy Sisters asked us for a dime or so:
For each gift, color one brick on white chart, was the rule.
    I put mine lone on a much higher row;
Then, shamed, grabbed two bucks from our kitchen table
    To fill the blank; the nun my mama quickly phoned
"Had she approved being so charitable ?"
    What could poor Mom say ? "Well, go ahead".
    Condoned, I filled the twenty blanks in red
While razor-strop at home was being honed.

    With cousin Bill I made my First Communion;
    We had a festive family reunion.
"Bill chewed the Host", I snitched; my mom and his were
peeved The men haw-hawed; said pastor not the least bit grieved:
    "That boy will be a priest; his piety
    Impedes no moralizing scrutiny'.

We moved to St. Cecilia's bounds;
         Sinsinawa Dominicans now teachers
            But with a two mile walk if straight each way
Plus detour prescribed avoiding railway grounds.
            They had me lead the Rosary at Mass through May.
Contests were favored by my lawyer dad for "Public Speech"-ers,
            And by the nuns, officially "Order of Preachers".
Each report card "Application C, deportment D"; rest A.
            Piano for a while; and "Palmer Method" hand:
My writing was so dreadful I preferred hand-print of poster.
            For homework or exams to be turned in, and
         (Plain fact; not to be a boaster)
This lettering-mania proved a useful bribe through strife
            Of longish years of academic life.

Creighton Prep: though I was too young for my classes
            Quite won my heart, and Jesuit teachers youngish too.
One genius made First Latin endless games: baseball and passes.
            Others made algebra , poetry and Greek the thing to do.
After school I stopped at public Tech to learn my typing;
But for my Jesuit role-models had never any griping.

2. SAINT LOUIS 1931-1945

Near the town to which in pioneer days were sent a flurry
            Of letters for "Saint Louis, near Florissant, Missouri"
            Our first-year novice group was sixty strong,
A real"Boys' Town" of population hundred twenty
With forty second-year and "Brothers" plenty,
            In all four hundred, if you count along

The graduates to "classics" and older "providers"'
We "city boys" out in the country were isolated outsiders.
    The peak year; eight thousand Jesuits in the U.S.A.,
      Dwindled to less than four thousand today.

After some four-five years: to Saint Louis. What a change!
Big University in center of a top metropolis
      And a range
Of confreres from N'yorleans, West Coast, N'York megalopolis.

    Our Sunday walks up Lindell past Museum's Forest Park
To posh rival university's campus in position
Of'Meet me in Saint Louie, Louie" Exposition.

    Three years of youthful manhood, a real lark.
They called our gang "Philosophers", Aquinas not Descartes,
But it meant chiefly "College Course":science and art.

Theology and Ordination, by academic rule
    Part of the Saint Louis U. connection,
Shortly before had moved to famed "Tom Playfair" school,
    Saint Marys Kans, where later we'd rejoin our groups
      For four years "isolated rejection"
    (That too now changed by murmur of the troops).

    Saint Louis, though the city too has dwindled far,
    Retains its charm as its alumni's guiding star.

3. MILWAUKEE 1939-41

Summers from Saint Louis to North Wisconsin situation
    Gave first glimpse of Milwaukee's splendid placing.
When time came to disperse through Province schools
    For this hid preference my heart was racing
And won !Marquette High to teach Greek/Latin rules
And hush study-hall and chapel turmoil of a younger generation;
Plays ticket-manager, then changed to Flambeau school paper:
    Two brightest years of a happy life's long caper.

Twenty years later, meanwhile transferred
    To new Milwaukee-centered jurisdiction,
Random terms in Marquette U. theology now spurred
    Concern for college youth, in painful friction
        Of the late sixties global, then milder days
        For Second Vatican our hopes to raise.

            With finally"the last of life
            For which the first was made"
A new millennium would begin with lush Medicare aid,
            Beyond challenge and strife
At Camillus Jesuit retirement community
With easy access burgeoning Marquette-zone cynosures to see.

4. ROME 1946 - 2000

Stuck in New York a month by strikers of the foam,
    Last minute Air France flight to Paree Gay
    Night train, no food, due in Rome next day.
But Italian border: food-bargaining, bridges bombed, delay;
    Ill-starred arrival rain and dark--but"Welcome home!"
    In city center, near new Gregorian, Biblico survivors
Held out indeed warm welcome to first post-war arrivers
Next day, again in rain and dark, glimpsed Tiber, Peters dome.
Then to work, no books or clothes till trunk arrived months late,
Mid European mates (teen-slaveys for Italian practice great).

Hebrew-cognate Arabic allured beyond the line of duty
(No thought of future use or strife) just for its beauty.
    But mostly class, with genial rector Bea to warn
Against Wellhausen, Second Isaiah, and such innovations.
Between picture-charm Egyptian and grim Babylonian torn:
All in Latin, confusing "same yet different" Italian aspirations.
    Third year: classes done, doctorate theme chosen,
The normal moment came for mid-East Bible lands tour.
    I had to try it all by myself, so inoperatively frozen
    Were tourist-aids by new state Israel's danger-whirr.

Meanwhile summers in France, Germany, and Spain
    Libraries and languages filled needs for dissertation.
Hand-typed four carbon-copies, all settled in the main.
Then off to Oxford, Avon, Erin awaiting evaluation.
Back Romeward for defense and packing:
But suddenly an archeology prof was lacking;
They told me "Start this fall"; Saint Louis must wait,
    Or get a better biblist for its theologate.

Ironic: teaching *dernier cri* archeology in language dead! Latin
    had terms for Rome's Mid-East geography,
But for pairing Hebrew toponyms Arabic was still best instead.
    Headaches reading exams in hundredfold calligraphy.
        Exciting times for Vatican displeasure
        Sidelining teachers by Modernism measure.
          For fringe-involvement even I, some said,
        Was exiled the Jerusalem branch to head,
And excavate its Dead Sea site, till things died down,
When a new Pope restored the profs of more renown.

        Latin by then had died a natural death
        Inevitable: but sad to see transformed
          To an Italian enterprise what first took breath
        As Extraterritorial, 'twere but by Latin normed.
    From Russ-dominated Poland we got dozens.
(Some summers, only there, communism left quite free
To travel, and thus gain some Polish skills for me.)
Slavs mourned Latin, yet enhanced our status "all-nations",
Rome's too, with epochalnon-Italian Pope and Slavic cousins.
    Invited Scholars from far raised Biblico reputations.

"Palestinology' from two to one semester flung,
    Alternate Latin-English too, till it emerged
The English option drew non-Anglophones to learn our tongue,
While "my Italian"drew Inglesi as bridge to what more
urged."Retirement"
at Elenchus editor's death would consist
In my "filling in awhile", toil congenial I'd not resist.

5. PALESTINE 1949-1976

Early in a first three-month Jerusalem stay
With new-drawn Arab-Israel frontiers
     For smaller Bible sites, the easiest way
     To get a needed permit was to say
"Archeologist !", partly at least true, quickly clears
The path to excavations: most with Bible names, near borders.
     Unguardedly writing about this to Rome
Determined future archeology teaching orders.
Now: retreat, Last Vows at Calvary, Egypt ere turning home.

With ASOR help, back for Kenyon enterprise at Jericho,
Then Byblos for a summer near Jesuit Lebanon college
     Meantime semesters, learning more than teaching, so
To gain in books &in the field ancient-lore knowledge.
     More field-work thanks to Orientalia German editor's pull
A chance at famed Boghazk"y amid the Turks
     Then Uruk-Warka near Ur/Babel, with a lull
For Persian Susa and Persepolis my camera lurks.

Already after Jericho veered to a new vocation:
     Annual thirty priest-prof study tour to organize,
With Sidon, Palmyra, Sinai, Luxor, Petra: every nation
     Where Arabic was needed; then Israel as prize;
     Not only student-priests' sheer gratitude to win,
     Also Rome courses to enrich with latest spin.
In intervals, modern Hebrew learn and teach,
And World-Jewish meetings archeo-exegesis update reach.

6. AUSTRALIA 1963

While captaining Jerusalem branch, some whole semesters
      For smaller group, to study Dead Sea text,
Then for exam, from Scrolls themselves in Museum to read.
One of these eager-beaver proto-Hebrew testers,
      Returning to Down Under homeland next,
         Heard "canonical visitation" plead:
Sydney must get short-term theologians from abroad.
        Boldly he put forward his ex-teacher's name
        And so for want of better, down I came.
Taught a semester Scripture without actual fraud.

      The English spoken in those groves of Academe
Was irreproachable, far better than "Amurrican" or Leeds;
      But once or twice in downtown crowds I'd seem
      To hear "Strine" sounds of quite different breeds.
Yet all felt they at once the kindness owed me,
      Quickly to shift to Oxfordese to help the stranger.
My Olympic-victor lady-pilot o'er the outback showed me
      How fly and land a Cessna in one easy lesson sans danger.

Desperately I strove to meet some proto-Australian folk
      Formerly called "Abo", unresisting shy
      Unlike New Zealand's self-asserting thriving Maori.
All I could find were west of Darwin, not in joke
Called ex-Jesuit leper mission, but too tamed.
And in Papua, oft by anthropologists named.

Lectured all over if invited, or else exploring wandered,
Even in New Zealand and Fiji some time squandered.
      Returning from Down Under via Jakarta
      And Indonesian Buruduru and Jokjakarta.
Then: exiled Chinese Mission in Viet-Nam (a week before our
                                  war,

And Diem and Kennedy assassinations scary)
Filipino Cebu too; lightwork a month in Baguio;
Kansas confreres revisiting in Zamboanga, Molokai, and so
Via Okinawa brother's post to Hiroshima's evil star
And brief salute to our new Kwang-Ju Seminary.

7. KOREA 1965 & 1978

That was the caper fraught with unforeseen
But not unwelcome outcome,"Back to Kwang-Ju next year".
Ten months still mid Rome/Mid-East routine,
To grab a toehold on Chinese-sign language, and prepare
Class-outlines sent ahead to be put in Korean
And English columns, for first class-day ready.
Local tutor's patient skill to share his tongue so heady
Tenth of what young Jesuits learned in struggles herculean.

The alphabet is easier far
Than Japanese, but most sounds are
Equal to dozen Chinese signs and meanings.
Teacher in speaking would trace sign in air
Or quick erase it if with uncertain leanings.
So easy to read aloud in unison a prayer,
Tyro's transcribing deemed blasphemous and unfair.

Our youthful Christians seemed attached to Latinizing;
Preferred baptismal Eusebius to common Pak, Lee, Kim;
It almost verged on old-style churchly colonizing:
"Bread of Life" flamed in chapel, flag or hymn
Where daily life-giver was only rice,
Bread an imported "let them eat cake" device.
Catholic churches were like fortresses of armed cement
While "meeting-houses" had a humbler friendly-garden bent.

Our students diligently learned their religion,
     In English, seeming almost more important to them.
One wrote "Three points: first ball"--a smidgeon
       Of their Americanization. All respect is due them
         For clinging to their faith of martyrs' blood
         But indignation would stream out like a flood
If challenged:"Yours is a faith of your own continent, Asia;
       Be proud of that; don't let it faze you;
Not something Greek from Rome via London and California:
We look to Jesus' Semite-Syrian scene: let that adorn you".

       At Seoul Sogang University a week
         Of lectures; only twelve years later
       A full semester, in English mostly so to "speak",
         But studies of some problems newly greater,
       Translated, some published in Korean dress.
Hearing famed preachers, half-earphoned half without.
       Mingling with lively populace-excess.
New friends, though U.S./S.J. control was headed out.

       Finally back to Rome on Transiberian; stops excite:
Novosibirsk, observing salesladies all day in open air
       At 45 below, point where Centigrade is Fahrenheit;
At hero-shrine boys stand guard outdoors an hour in pair.

       Train-rails relaid across a frozen lake;
       Cross Urals onto European soil.
A week in Moscow; Kremlin, opera, ballet Bolshoi to take;
       Subway with stained glass, real cathedral of atheist toil;

Long on-train chat with Viet-Nam student-guest agreeably
Eager to speak known tongue even with his "enemy".

Communist train-welcomers and guides helpful though spyingly.
Courteous except at borders(all foodstuffs confiscated
                           Tit-for-tat to U.S. policy).
Last Kiev, Odessa and (without off-limits Yalta) Black Sea.

          At Czech border, Russian guards invade
          Fiercely drive others out whose seats were paid;
      Each item of my baggage fling about
In search of contraband Bibles ! (though going out).

8. ELENCHUS 1980-2000

Rome's Institute was funded for biblical library superfine.
      The single cataloguer began a simple "list"
         Of acquisitions, which roused interest.
      As bibliography by scholarship sore missed.
It took on proportions too great for mere sideline.
      My German classmate, Peter Nober, 1950 named
         To full-scale production, was instantly acclaimed
Throughout the world indispensable for the Word divine.

ELENCHUS! One must wonder how Greek for
                          "disgraceful shames",
      Perhaps via "cross-examining, investigation" as today,
Came to mean in Latin simply "list of names"
Elenchus Bibliographicus biblicus its title we must say;
Subheads too Latin; but contents every language under heaven,
      Thousand-page annual, a worldwide leaven:
      "What's not in Nober just does not exist" was said.
      I'd helped proofread the languages alive and dead,
But was en route to Korea for announced third stay
      When phoned from Rome: "Come back: emergency!
Nober has cancer; get his materials and rules of play,
      And fill in while about replacement we see."

A week later back in Munich for the last farewell.
   One volume was just ready for the press,
Next hundred thousand slips still to be typed pell-mell
   (In Nober-era all handwritten, with what stress!).
   It was a thrilling toil for a frustrated language-buff
Prepared by stays in Mid-E ast, Turkey, Sweden, Hungary,
          Poland too,
For swoops on Rome's fine French, German, Vatican research
stuff,
Saint Louis and Milwaukee libraries the summers through.
   Elenchus of Biblica it became, though nearly sued,
Or faced with fine or prison for alleged changed-title fix,
   (Nober's for ten years could Elenchus in Biblica include):
Scholarship may be sometimes at odds with law or politics.

Full fifteen years, till could be found successor steady.
Computer, miraculous but slow to learn, emerged to aid:
For last three volumes hundred-page Index camera-ready
And final year entire, though half by Althann made.

9. WAUWATOSA 2000

In Rome from all other duties in escape
   A gracious Rector suggested free-time help
To put the dusty Archives and his own files in shape
But I felt that both the troops and higher-ups would yelp
    If our famed Institutes seemed like Old People's Homes
      To needed and prospective young recruits
      For forwarding their pioneering fruits,
    And win the public by more updated tomes.
Impelled by guilty conscience to agree,
I gave in to Milwaukee's new retirement community.

Arriving at suburban Wauwatosa, Camillus East fourth floor,
    I felt content and peaceful, "home at last",
Amid other octogenarians a score,
Some, a mite reluctant, some delighted more;
        Glad once-congenial travel-days were past.
    Irrelevant and unforeseen were the attractions
Of Medicare and all the billions spent
By our undoubtedly vote-thirsty government,
    But playing a mammoth role in our satisfactions.

Retirees notoriously, usually much younger,
    Are bored and itchy for "something to do".
Beyond prayer-duties and satisfying hunger
    Or blessed TV and the daily "What's new ?"
I had at once a fine computer (though
    Most comrades had none or but rarely used);
    Also a Rome-destined Hebrew learner, abused
As skilled technician showing all I need to know.

For mornings that sufficed; then till bedtime from noon
    Shakespeare, Grisham, Westerns, mysteries, Scott:
    With quick bus-access to libraries, Public and Marquette:
Thus passed one whole year congenial; but I soon
    Missed some serious research-reading, and could not
    Foresee a future with no project over which to fret.

As asthma, deafness, stumbling pace forebode to hold me down
    I got the wild idea that Poetry was most suited
To room-bound menace, and wrote verses "What a clown
    Without due preparation !" at myself I hooted.
So gathered, copied, re-learned a hundred college-day
    Favorites in rhyme and meter; tried to see
    Why nothing now is "in" except the "verse that's free".

Poetaster never published, that's okay,
I tried to feel; but no poem is really complete
Unless the critic public judgment it can meet.
Unmoved by fame or money, is it worth the strain
To keep on trying, with no prospects new ?
A way out day by day I sought "in vain ?"
Not really, since it was something worth-while to do.

Finito di stampare
nel mese di Giugno 2004

presso la tipografia
"Giovanni Olivieri" di E. Montefoschi
00187 Roma • Via dell'Archetto, 10, 11, 12
Tel. 06 6792327 • E-mail: tip.olivieri@libero.it